FOREWORD

One of the key qualities that makes some soldiers more efficient with their fighting 'skills' against a determined enemy is 'morale'. This extra confidence was boosted by happier moments out of the field of battle, tinged with humour, laughter, comradeship and temporary peace, and this was undeniably achieved by Ray Harris over several years and recalled so lovingly in Jenny Hall's evocative book *A Desert Rat Entertains*.

Most divisions did not have the happy luxury of a professional troupe from within their ranks. The Desert Rats were a stronger, certainly more confident formation through Ray Harris' untiring efforts. They were Winston Churchill's favourite division and in his memoirs he made that absolutely clear. He would certainly have approved and applauded Ray Harris' skills, humour and talent.

Patrick Delaforce
RHA Troop Commander 1945-1948,
commanding Java Troop

Preface

After my mother died, in 2006, I came across all the letters my father had written to her during the Second World War. They were hidden in an old chocolate box, the lid of which she had inscribed:

'My happy dreams are stored away
The happy dreams of yesterday
A tender message to impart
When it is winter in the heart
And dreams of you, like summer flowers
Steal back to fill the empty hours
Recapturing old ecstasies
With ever fragrant memories.'

Doreen Sellman

Prelude

Both my parents had fathers who could be described as 'showmen'.

This is how *The World's Fair* (7 November 1970) described my mother Doreen's father, Arthur Sellman:

> *A native of Cannock, Staffordshire, as a young man Arthur travelled the fairgrounds widely as projectionist and lecturer on the early Bioscope Shows ... He was later engaged in puppet and marionette shows, in connection with which he made his own figures. At the outbreak of the 1914–1918 war, Arthur was entertaining the troops in Norfolk. He also had connections with the circus and did much advance work. He later turned his attention to the permanent cinema ... the Princes' Theatre at Brighton which he managed for 13 years.*

Arthur was a correspondent of *The World's Fair* for over 50 years. He wrote under the name 'Southdown'.

My father Ray's father, Frank Harris, appears in an article written by 'Southdown' in *The World's Fair* (14th January 1933):

> *I was pleased to receive a call last week from my old friend Mr. Frank Harris whose show under the above title is touring with success. His son* [Ray] *is principal clown and his daughter Vera is doing a clever balancing act. They are en route for the West Country.*

Arthur Sellman ('Southdown'), Doreen's father.

Elizabeth Sellman, Doreen's mother.

It was a Mr. Henderson (whose death *The World's Fair* announced on 15 July 1932) who was indirectly responsible for bringing my parents together. He '*died suddenly on the roadside at Bucklebury Common on the morning of 6th July ... 60 years of age and had been in the circus business for 41 years and he was at Bramber Castle for the last two years.*'

Frank Harris, Ray's father.

In 1930 Arthur Sellman made one of his frequent attempts to make the family fortune. He placed two wolves in a cage in the grounds of Bramber Castle as part of the 'Henderson Circus'.[1] My mother, Doreen, aged ten, dressed in a uniform, sold tickets.

Doreen Sellman, Brighton 1932.

1 The Henderson Circus is mentioned on the Beatles' *Sgt. Pepper's Lonely Hearts' Club Band* album, on the track 'Being for the Benefit of Mr. Kite'.

The Harris family were also at Bramber with Mr. Henderson, as one journalist wrote '*quietly jogging along and getting a good living*.' Ray was 16 and it was with his sister Vera that Doreen immediately struck up a friendship. Ray, six years Doreen's senior, pushed her on the swing in Bramber Castle Grounds.

Rex Morrison, Ray's friend.

When the Harris family left Bramber they went back on the road with their show. Four years passed and Vera, on holiday in Brighton with her Auntie Mary, met Doreen, with her father and mother, along the London Road. Instead of going to the Hippodrome show as planned, the Sellman family spent the evening with Vera and Auntie Mary in the 'Baby's Bar'.

Following that evening, Frank Harris got in touch with Arthur Sellman again. Over the next few years the two families would reunite at Christmas and Doreen gave Ray a few dancing lessons (mentioned in future correspondence).

In 1938, the Harris family stopped travelling and settled in Charlotte Street in Brighton. Doreen had left school at 14 and was managing a sweet shop called the 'Candy Box' in Air Street. Ray would often come into the shop with his friend Rex for a few Woodbine cigarettes on their way to Sherry's, a popular dance hall just off the sea front.

When war was declared in 1939, the Sellman family moved to Cannock in Staffordshire to live with Arthur's sister. Ray was called up in June 1940.

Events Leading to the Second World War

Whilst the previous events were taking place, it was becoming clear that Hitler was developing his vision of Germany as world master. It was set out in his publication in the 1920s of *Mein Kampf* ('My Struggle'). Germany's great economic crisis, following its defeat in the First World War, was fertile ground for cultivating such aspirations.

In March 1936, Hitler defied the Treaty of Versailles by moving his army into the Rhineland and refortifying his western frontier. Britain and France's policy was one of appeasement. Neither wanted another war and both felt that Hitler was preferable to Communism, which he opposed.

By 1937, Hitler had built a considerable army and air force, bigger and more modern than Britain's. In November of that year, at a secret conference in Berlin, Hitler revealed his plan to conquer Poland and the USSR by first taking Austria and Czechoslovakia. In March 1938, Austria was forced to unite with Germany and the Munich Conference allowed Hitler to take all the districts of German-speaking people in Czechoslovakia. When Hitler invaded Poland in September 1939, Britain, under Neville Chamberlain, France and the Dominions of the British Commonwealth declared war on Germany.

During the winter of 1939/1940 there was no land fighting in France and Britain. Both countries worked hard to build up their armed forces. In order to strengthen his position against Britain, Hitler invaded Denmark and Norway in April

1940. On 10 May Holland and Belgium were invaded and Winston Churchill took over from Neville Chamberlain.

In order to help the Belgians, Britain advanced from the Franco-Belgian frontier but, whilst this advance was in progress, the Germans attacked through unprotected Luxembourg. The British Army and some French became trapped between the sea and the German Army, now at the mouth of the River Somme. The British and French were picked up at Dunkirk and brought safely back to England by a fleet of small boats.

France surrendered on 22 June 1940. Ten days before, Italy, under Mussolini, had also declared war on France and Britain. Italy wanted to seize colonies in North Africa.

It was in June 1940, as a result of all these developments, that Ray was called up. He was sent for training to Perham Down in Hampshire.

Chapter 1

AT PERHAM DOWN

Vera had suggested that Doreen should write to 'Son', the family name for Ray. He had been at Perham Down nearly five months before he answered her first letter.

L/CPL R.A.J. Harris 7911536,
39 Squad 'A' Squadron,
54th A.T.R. R.A.C.,
Perham Down,
(Near Andover),
Hants.

23.10.40.

Dear Doreen,
I am so sorry that I have not answered your letter before but I have been up to my neck in work. Well! How are you all? It seems ages since I saw you. What a rotten war this is isn't it? Although I don't find the army life too bad. I am expecting another stripe soon and I am training to be a foot drill instructor ...
Well Doreen please write to me when you can find time ...
With love,
Son.

As well as preparing for battle, Ray was busy rehearsing the 'Odds and Ends' concert party. On 28 August 1940, he had contributed to a number called *Strumming* and on 18 September 1940 to another called *He'll Never Change.*

Further correspondence from that time seems to have petered out. A Christmas card survives from 1940, the verse of which concludes:

There's one to whom
A special wish I send –
Good fortune and the best of cheer
Bring joy to you my friend
With love,
From
Son.

Whilst Ray was training at Perham Down, a grave situation had been developing. In August and September 1940, the Battle of Britain was fought in the air over Southern England and the English Channel. Hitler's aim was to kill off the RAF. By so doing, the German air force would be free to protect their invasion transports from the British Navy. By a very narrow margin, Britain won. Churchill said: *'Never in the field of human conflict was so much owed by so many to so few.'*

Although Hitler stopped the immediate invasion of England, the winter of 1940/41 saw the bombing of London, Coventry, Birmingham, Plymouth, Liverpool, Bristol and Southampton. Britain's merchant ships suffered serious losses but, with the help of radar and the development of effective defence, Germany also started to suffer losses. Italy, now an enemy, put pressure on Britain's resources as Britain was already fighting against German fighter aircraft and submarines.

Ray's squadron. Ray marked by a cross.

Christmas card sent to Doreen from Ray, 1940.

Chapter 2

Northern Africa

Nearly a whole year passed and there appears to have been no communication between Ray and Doreen (now 21). Ray was posted at the end of 1940 to Egypt where he served in the 7th Armoured Division of the 8th Army, known as the Desert Rats. He was a tank driver and involved in all the Western Desert Campaigns.

He also joined a concert party called 'The Jerboa Strollers'. Newspaper cuttings from the time state:

> *It was the first front line concert party to be formed from the troops of a British Armoured Division. The settings for their desert performances are pretty rough and, if it's too late after the show to go home, they sleep in the sand around their props truck. Their piano was on one occasion completely demolished by a bomb.*

Mussolini intended to invade Egypt from the Italian colony of Libya. His aim was to prevent the British from using the Suez Canal. The government agreed to send weapons, including heavy tanks, to the British Army in Egypt. By June 1940, the Italian Army was on the Egyptian frontier. Two hundred and fifteen thousand Italians were against only the 7th Armoured Division, the infantry brigade in Mersa Matruh and the 4th Indian Division. War was declared against Italy on 11 June 1940. By the time Ray was posted to

Egypt in December 1940, the offensive was already under way, despite a shortage of men, artillery, tanks and motor transport. The tank that Ray initially drove was almost certainly limited by wear in its tracks.

'The Jerboa Strollers' 1941. Ray (left), Harry Ball (centre), Ronnie Vaughan (right).

On 8 December 1940, the Division began its attack on the Italian 10th Army which had advanced into Egypt as far as Sidi Barrani.

In a number of encircling manoeuvres, the Italians were pursued westwards. Sidi Barrani was captured on 16 December 1940, Bardia on 1 January 1941 and Tobruk 22 January 1941.

At the Battle of Beda Fomm, on 6–7 February 1941, the Italian Army was completely destroyed. Afterwards, the tanks in Ray's brigade consisted of 39 intact, 48 damaged by artillery fire, 8 disabled, 1 caught fire and 8 broken down (altogether 101 tanks).

The 7th Arm'd Div. had travelled 150 miles across unmapped desert.

The Desert Rats, although outnumbered by the enemy and despite a serious lack of water, food, petrol and ammunition, had beaten a force ten times stronger than themselves without any extra air support.

At the end of February 1941, the Division drove into Cairo victorious. It then spent some time resting, refitting (with some American supplies) and retraining before facing an expected German onslaught. America, under Roosevelt, in January 1941 had agreed to supply Britain with weapons, food and raw materials without payment.

During the week leading up to the end of March, the German army was building up in Tripolitania. By the beginning of April, the German offensive started at El Agheila.

The British re-equipment was taking longer than expected. Tank repairs were slow and when a tank-carrying convoy arrived it had lost a quarter of the tanks. By the start of May there were only two completed operational units of both Cruiser and 'I' tanks. The tank crews, Ray being one of their members, would have been getting used to the new vehicles. It was hoped they would be ready by June.

From 15 to 20 June 1941 Operation Battleaxe took place. Its object was to beat the enemy in the Western Desert and force it back west of Tobruk. The 7th Arm'd Div. had about

200 tanks and it was the first occasion on which it faced the Germans in a full-scale tank battle. It met with little success.

1. El Krib
2. Tunis
3. Medenine
4. Tarhuna
5. Tripoli
6. Tripolitania
7. Homs
8. El Agheila
9. Agedabia
10. Beda Fomm
11. Benghazi
12. Sidi Rezegh
13. Cyrenaica
14. Tobruk
15. Bardia
16. Sidi Azeiz
17. Sollum
18. Sidi Barrani
19. Mersa Matruh
20. El Alamein
21. Alexandria
22. Cairo
23. Alam Halfa Ridge

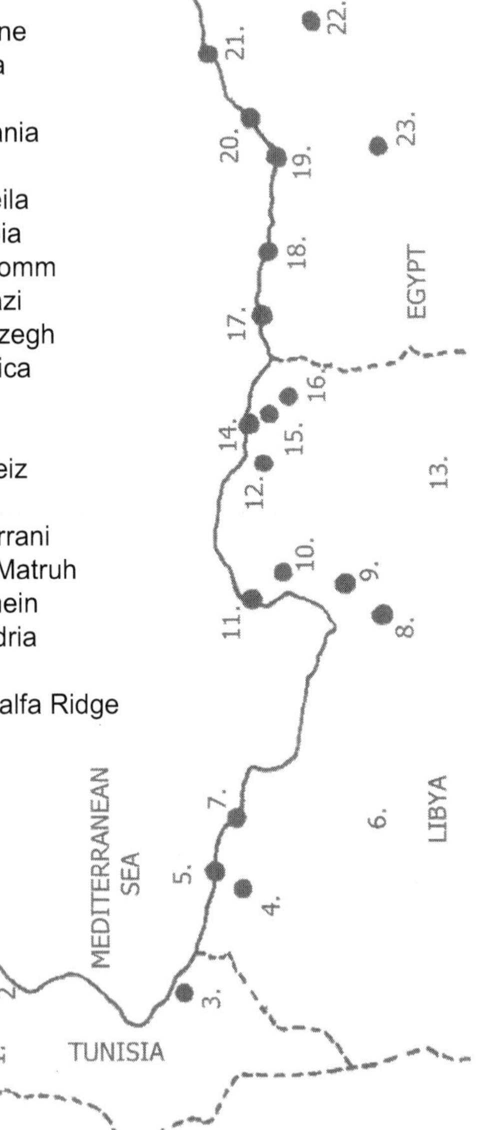

Sketch map of N. Africa

Many of the new cruiser tanks called 'Crusaders' had two-pounder guns but failed to live up to expectation. Although they were quick, they were unreliable. The guns had little power or range. The German tanks could knock out the British at 2,000 yards, whereas the cruisers had a shorter range of 600–800 yards. Many broke down before being knocked out. From 15–17 June the battle lasted 72 hours. Despite the unsuccessful outcome, German manoeuvres (apart from at Tobruk) were prevented. Most of the 7th Arm'd Div. withdrew to the area south of Matruh.

The next four months proved to be quiet. Tank losses had to be made up and the armoured units were re-equipped and retrained.

Troops were then moved to a small area near a railway station called El Alamein, 60 miles from Alexandria.

Whilst these events were taking place, Hitler was attacking Russia. He withdrew his attention from Britain for the time being. It is generally accepted that this attack cost him the war.

In November 1941 a series of attacks were launched called Operation Crusader, the purpose of which was to destroy the German and Italians' armour, recapture Cyrenaica and relieve Tobruk. The first phase took place between 18 and 23 November. The battle raged around Sidi Rezegh (important for its airfield and northern ridge which overlooked Tobruk).

The Germans attacked relentlessly with vast numbers of heavy tanks. There was much gallantry from the 7th Arm'd Div. but also many casualties. Its vehicles and guns were inferior to the enemy's and the tanks were reduced to a handful (one of which was driven by Ray).

There is some doubt as to whether Ray was involved in the active combat of the second and third phases. A poster advertising 'Jerboa Strollers on Parade. A non-stop Variety Show featuring Ray Harris' at the Garrison Opera House, Abbassia dates the performance as Tuesday 2 December

1941. On the other hand, the second phase of Operation Crusader (24 November–1 December 1941) resulted in more heavy losses on both sides. There was great difficulty in identifying both men and vehicles as all had been covered in dust from the desert. It would seem unlikely that Ray would have been exempted from taking part in order to prepare for a variety show.

The third phase (2–10 December 1941) saw the enemy withdraw from the Tobruk perimeter. By this time the 7th Arm'd Div. was utterly exhausted. Many had been fighting for three weeks and, had they been armed with better tanks and guns, more lives would have been saved.

During the last phase of Crusader (11–27 December 1941) Cyrenaica was recaptured from the enemy, and on 3 January 1942 the Division rested near Cairo. Its part in these winter manoeuvres ended at this point. It wasn't until the beginning of April 1942 that it returned to the desert for training southwest of Sidi Azeiz.

Throughout these events in December 1941, Hitler had failed to destroy the Russian armies and the German army had suffered greatly from the severe Russian winter. On 7 December 1941, the Japanese attack on the American Pacific Fleet at Pearl Harbour in the Hawaiian Islands brought America into the war against Japan and Germany.

On December 20 1941, Ray performed in cabaret at an official staff dinner. Jasper Maskelyne, the famous stage illusionist and magician, introduced him and continued to present many shows. Eager to participate in the war effort, Maskelyne had trained at camouflage school. Posted to Egypt in 1941, he played an influential part in various deceptive strategies such as creating dummy tanks and other false war material (some on a considerable scale).

HEADQUARTERS CAIRO AREA

Staff Dinner

Saturday December 20th 1941

DINNER 8.00 p.m.
CABARET 9.30 p.m.

Programme cover for the staff dinner and cabaret presented by Jasper Maskelyne, December 20 1941.

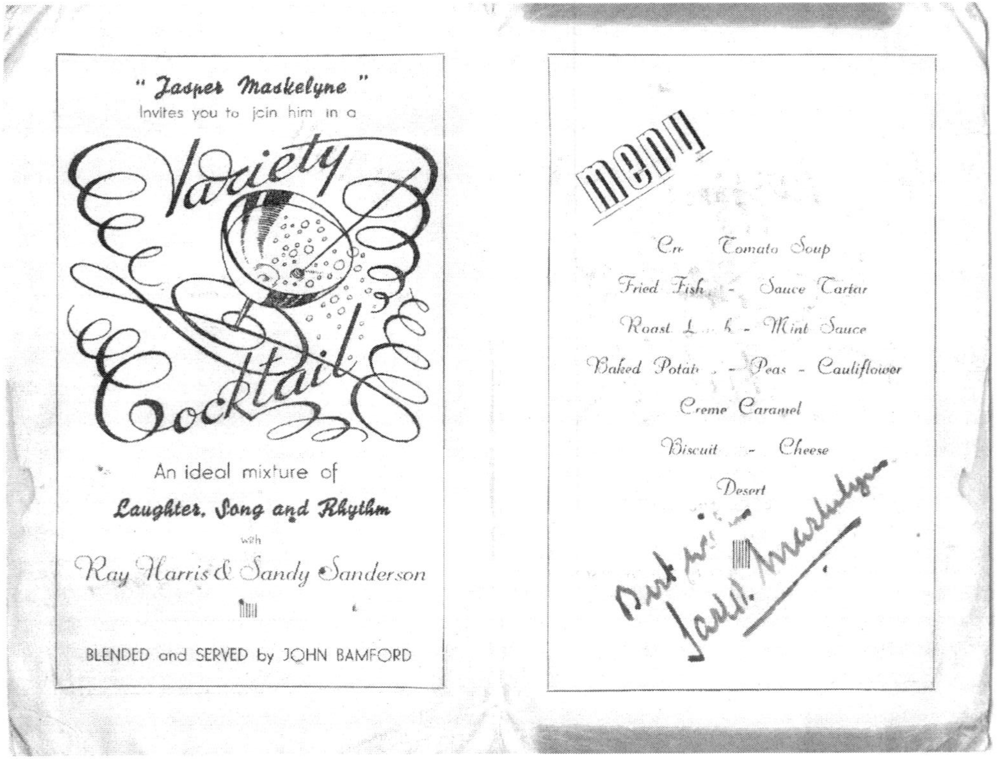

"Jasper Maskelyne"
Invites you to join him in a

Variety Cocktail

An ideal mixture of
Laughter, Song and Rhythm
with
Ray Harris & Sandy Sanderson

BLENDED and SERVED by JOHN BAMFORD

MENU

Cr. Tomato Soup
Fried Fish - Sauce Tartar
Roast L... b - Mint Sauce
Baked Potat.. - Peas - Cauliflower
Creme Caramel
Biscuit - Cheese
Desert

Best wi...
Jasper Maskelyne

Inside of the programme for the staff dinner and cabaret presented by Jasper Maskelyne, December 20 1941.

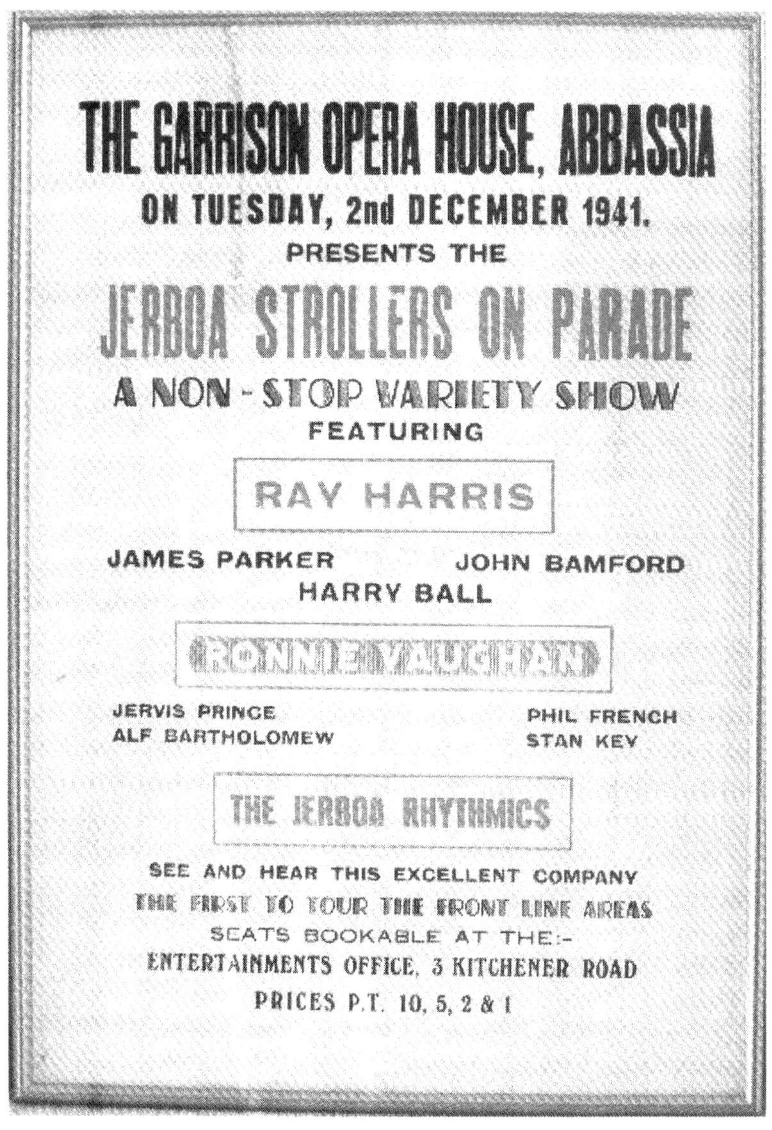

The poster advertising Ray's performance at the Garrison Opera House, Abbassia on 2 December 1941

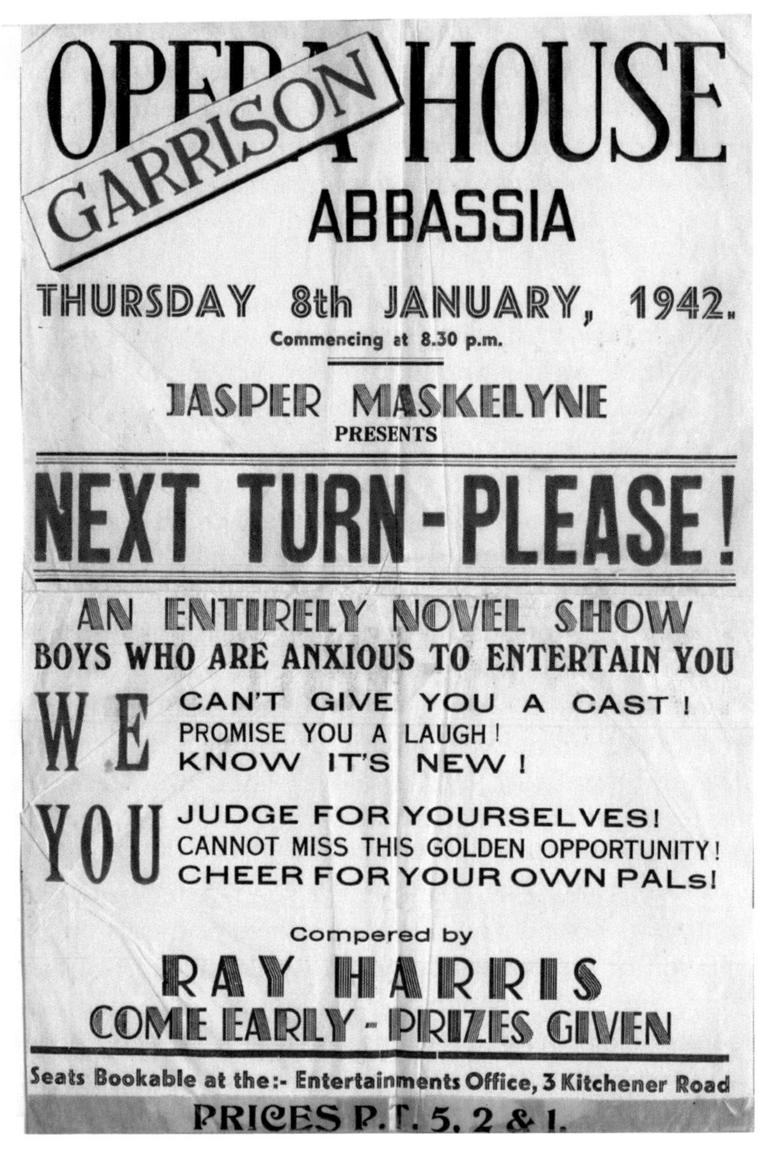

The poster advertising Ray's appearance at the Garrison Opera House in a show presented by Jasper Maskelyne on 8 January 1942.

Ray's service medals.

The value of the welcome distraction from the horrors of war offered by the concert parties cannot be overestimated. Ray's contribution to the 'Jerboa Strollers' performances is immortalised in posters advertising those at the Opera House Abbassia and newspaper cuttings (from 2 December 1941 and 8 January 1942).

The following review is typical:

> *The star comedian of the show put on at Abbassia which was allegedly watered down for the benefit of the fair sex present in the audience was Ray Harris. Mr. Harris has a perfect, polished patter, all of his own making; at least the present writer had never heard any of the stories before. He appeared variously as a drunk, as cupid (in large army issue boots) and what is known as an eccentric comedian, we believe. He was grand in this last role. He had the theatre rocking from the moment he made his entry.*

Another letter, undated, seems to have been written very soon after the first from the desert.

> *Dear Doreen,*
> *... So you are working in a grocery store eh? I should love to see Miss Sellman. I expect she brings sunshine and happiness to every customer doesn't she? ... I suppose I feel a bit jealous about the boyfriends I hear about. I hope they are not around when I come for that picture date or else – ! ... I hope you will write to me often and look upon me as a boyfriend as well ...*
> *x x x x x x Yours always,*
> *Son.*
> ↑
> *I hope these make the boyfriends jealous.*

As stated in the last letter, Doreen was now working in a grocer's in Cannock in the Midlands. She was soon to be called up to work in Guest, Keen and Nettlefolds' factory.

Two short airgraphs follow dated 1 June 1942 and 11 June 1942.

In the next letter Ray mentions some radio broadcasts at the ESB[2] Studio. A contemporary news cutting states:

'On Thursday they come to the E.S.B. Studio to entertain the troops again, this time in the Forces Programme – before they go back to their armoured division. The names of those taking part in the broadcast are Ray Harris ...'

During the weary months of waiting in the desert the Jerboa Strollers had over 200 performances.

Ray, entertaining at Jerboa Bay (near Tobruk, Libya), May 1942.

2 Egypt State Broadcasting

13.6.42.

My dear Doreen,

Today has been a lucky day for me as I have just received two letters from you dated 26/3/42 and 2/4/42. Thanks a lot dear. I also celebrate my two years in the army today ... This war has certainly taught me a lesson. I think I shall settle down to home life after all this.

The Army sobers you up a bit and makes you realize that there is much more in life than just going out with a different girl every night and generally trying to paint the town red.

The old days seem so far away now don't they? Do you remember the first dancing lesson you gave me with the old gramophone scratching out 'Cheek to Cheek' rendered by the immortal Donald Peers? Still I think that there are a lot of happy days ahead of us don't you? Do you know dear, you are the only girl writing to me now. I do think of you a lot and look forward to your letters so much, so don't forget that date for the pictures when I get back and mind you're not late. We have just returned from another tour with the show. I would love you to see it ... We have a nice little band of piano, two sax's, violin, trumpet and drums. I am still doing my old Max Miller stuff and two or three songs. We have done one or two local broadcasts and are trying for a home relay.

If this does come off, I will send you a wire so that you can listen in to us. You haven't told me whether you have a boyfriend yet. I'm afraid that I'm going to be rather jealous if you have, so how about a photo of yourself and a real love letter? After all you are putting a lot of kisses in your letters and sticking the stamps on sideways so why not the real thing? And don't be shy. Must close now with fondest love and kindest regards to Mum and Dad. Please write again soon.

Ever yours,

Son. x x x x x x

28.6.42.

My dear Doreen,

I have just sent you off a bracelet … Well! How was old Brighton looking after so long. A funny thing happened the other day.

I was in a Y.M.C.A. here imbibing a cup of the local brew when one of the boys said to me, 'I bet you know that don't you?' and pointed to a picture on the wall. Sure enough there was Marine Parade in August. It certainly made me homesick for the rest of the day. By the way I saw a terrific film last month 'Moon Over Miami' with Betty Grable. See it if you get the chance, you will like it. Thanks very much for the photograph received last week, it is very nice … There isn't really much news this time and things are very quiet out here … with love and kisses, please write again soon.

Yours, Son. x x x x x x

(3)
trumpet + drums. I am still do-
-ing my old Max Miller stuff
and two or three songs. We have
done one or two local broadcasts,
+ are trying for a home relay.
If this does come off I will
send you a wire, so that you
can listen in to us. You haven't
told me whether you have a
boy friend yet. I'm afraid that I
am going to be rather jealous
if you have, so how about a
photo of yourself and a real love
letter, after you are putting a
lot of kisses in your letters +
sticking the stamps on sideways,
so why not the real thing?
+ don't be shy. Must close now
with fondest love + kindest regards
to mum + dad. Please write again
soon

ever yours
Son
xxxxxxx xxxxxxx
xxxxxxx xxxxxxx

AIR MAIL LETTER CARD

Miss D. Sellman,
33, Girton Road,
CANNOCK,
STAFFS,
Gt BRITAIN.

WHEN FOLDED THE LETTER CARD MUST CONFORM IN SIZE AND SHAPE WITH THE BLUE BORDER WITHIN WHICH THE ADDRESS ONLY MAY BE WRITTEN

EXAMINED BY BASE CENSOR

7911536. L/Cpl. Harris. R.A.J.
'Jerboa Strollers' Concert Pty
c/o 152 (Abbassia) Transit Camp
M.E.F.
13-6-42.

My dear Doreen,
Just a few lines once again. Today has been a lucky day for me as I have just received two letters from you dated 26/3/42 and 2/4/42, thanks a lot dear. I also celebrate my two years in the army today. time certainly does march on. I have been out here about sixteen months now, almost a native you might say. Yes I saw "The Great American Broadcast" out here last year, pretty good wasn't it? This war has certainly taught me a lesson, I think I shall settle down to home life after all this. The army sobers you up a bit, & makes you

(2)
realize that there is much more in life than just going out with a different girl every night & generally trying to paint the town red. The old days seem so far away now don't they? do you remember the first dancing lesson you gave me with the old gramophone scratching out "Cheek to Cheek" rendered by the immortal Donald Peers.
Still, I think that there are a lot of happy days ahead of us don't you? Do you know dear, you are the only girl writing to me now. I do think of you a lot & look forward to your letters so much so don't forget that 'date' for the pictures when I get back & mind you're not late. We have just returned from another tour with the show. I would love you to see it. Did Vera show you the bill I sent her. We have a nice little band of, piano, two sax's, violin,

One of Ray's letters to Doreen from N. Africa (13.06.1942).

Three days later Ray wrote a cablegram. It was the day German and Italian forces under Rommel launched an unsuccessful attack designed to capture El Alamein.

1.7.42.

My dear Doreen,
Your letters bring back so many happy memories for me. I look forward to them so much ... I have written to you three times this week and hope that you get them O.K., also the small gold and silver bracelet I sent. Yes, I am looking forward to us being all together again and reviving the old days. I do hope that it won't be long now. I meet quite a few Brighton chaps out here. The first thing they ask 'So you know Sherry's?'[3] 'Never heard of it!' Ha! Ha! Must close now, with fondest love & kisses. Please write again soon & God bless.
Son. x x x x x x

3 A popular dance hall in West Street, Brighton

Vera, Ray's sister, and his nephew Peter.

Eddie Lane, Vera's husband.

The next mentions a show.

23.7.42.

My dear Doreen,

Have just received two more letters from you and thanks a lot. I'm afraid that there isn't a great deal of news this time and things are very quiet.

We gave a show to the boys in a local N.A.F.F.I. last week, our first for many weeks. It went down very well and the hall was crowded, also another small 'write-up' in the local press. I see you mention 'Moon Over Miami' in your latest letter. I saw it a few weeks back and enjoyed it very much. I thought the techni colour was great didn't you? I received the photo of Vera[4] and the baby after all. I was beginning to think it had been lost. Anyway the baby looks grand. Imagine me an uncle. Ha! Ha!

By the sound of your letters you seem to be quite a 'super' film fan these days. We get quite a few decent films out here and I go whenever possible. I am so pleased to hear that you are all keeping O.K. The weather out here is getting very hot, but we are used to it by now. I don't know how the boys out here will manage after the war when they get back to 'Civvie Street' and England. I can picture myself with the old overcoat on in the middle of July ...

With fondest love and kisses,
Son. x x x x x x

There are then only two more letters before this period of comparative quiet comes to a close. The letters from this time on are signed 'Ray'.

1.8.42.

My dear Doreen,

... The weather here has been terribly hot this last few weeks, in fact the worst for many years, so the locals tell us.

At the moment of writing I am in the corporals' mess

4 Ray's sister Vera was now married to Eddie Lane

imbibing a bottle of iced beer, while Ambrose[5] *and his boys are knocking out 'Love is All'. Yes, the 'Strollers' are all keeping fine and the show continues to be most successful. The band are now featuring 'Apple Blossom Time' as their big number and very nice too, only I have nearly forgotten what apple blossom looks like. Do you think you really will be returning to Brighton when the war is over? I hope so ...*

Yours,
Ray.
xxxxxx

The following was the last letter Ray wrote before the Eighth Army had to face strong German and Italian forces under Rommel.

4.8.42.

My dear Doreen,

... I see by your latest airgraphs received yesterday that your dad managed to get a small 'write up' in the 'World's Fair'. Please thank him a lot for myself and the boys. Next Monday we hope to be on the 'air' again. N.A.A.F.I. want us to feature in their popular 'Radio Theatre' which is a local weekly variety item on the wireless out here. It is relayed from a big hospital, so we are looking forward to entertaining the boys. I would love you to see our No. 1 Show, especially Ronnie Vaughan our violinist and singing pianist. He is really terrific. If you prefer the accordion, Jimmy Barry will play you any number you like. Wally Adams is on the drums and boy, can he rattle those sticks! As a matter of fact, all the boys know their stuff and they should do after over 200 performances. I get a little tired of it all sometimes and can think of nothing except getting home.

Once I do, I don't think I shall ever want to move from the old easy chair. I wonder how it will all end? I often wonder don't you dear? Anyway we have a lot to make up for haven't we? I went to see Bing Crosby, Bob Hope and Dorothy Lamour in 'Road to Zanzibar' last night but was disappointed in it. You don't seem

5 Popular band leader of the time

to get really good numbers these days do you? Well dear I shall have to close again with love and kisses.

Hoping to hear from you soon dear.

Yours,

Ray x x x x x x x

In the next letter the 'Strollers' have been disbanded and preparations made for the Battle of Alam Halfa in early September when Rommel would try to break through the El Alamein line for a second time.

7911536. L/CPL. HARRIS. R.A.J.
"Jerboa Strollers" Concert Party
c/o 152 (Abbassia) Leave & Transit Camp
Middle East Forces.
4/8/42.

My dear Doreen,

Well! here are the photos as promised & I hope you will like them O.K.

I am posting this with an airmail lettercard, so you should receive them both pretty close together.

I see by your latest airgraph received yesterday that your dad managed to get a small write-up in the W.F. please thank him a lot for myself & the boys.

Next monday we hope to be on the air again. N.A.A.F.I. want us to feature in their popular "Radio Theatre" which is a local weekly variety item on the wireless out here. It is relayed from a big hospital, so we are looking forward

(2)

to entertaining the boys.

I would love you to see our No 1 show, especially Ronnie Vaughn our violinist & swing pianist, he is really terrific. If you prefer the accordion Jimmy Barry will play you any number you like.

Wally Adams is on the drums, & boy! can he rattle those sticks.

As a matter of fact, all the boys know their stuff, as they should do after over 200 performances.

I get a little tired of it all sometimes, & can think of nothing except getting home. Once I do, I don't think I shall ever want to move from the old easy chair.

I wonder how it will all end, I often wonder don't you dear? anyway we have a lot to make up for haven't we?

I went to see Bing Crosby, Bob Hope & Dorothy Lamour in "Road to Zanzibar" last night but was dissapointed in it. You

(3)

don't seem to get really good numbers these days do you? Well dear, I shall have to close once again with love & kisses

Hoping to hear from you soon dear.

Yours

Ray xxxxxx xxxxxx

xxxxxxxx xxxxxxxx

A letter from Ray describing 'The Jerboa Strollers'. (04.08.1942)

'The Jerboa Strollers' April 1942. Ray is in the centre.

7911 536 L/CPL HARRIS R.A.J.,
7th Armoured Division H.Q.,
M.E.H.

My dear Doreen,
You will probably be surprised to hear that 'The Strollers' have been temporarily disbanded. So the above will be my regular address until further notice. The party and myself are at present doing duty in the squadron. I am on my old job with the defence. Everybody here says that they are going to miss our shows and I think they will. They all looked forward to us during the weary months of waiting in the desert where we were the only party to tour the forward areas. A very prominent Lt. Colonel of the Division told us last year that we were worth a pound a minute to them, and when I saw the way with which our shows were received with such enthusiasm, from G.H.Q. to the smallest unit in the desert (from the officers and the boys), I was inclined to agree with him.

We can always rest assured that we have done our job and wherever the Div. have been we have been entertaining the lads. I do hope you receive the little present O.K. ...

Yours, Ray. x x x x x x

August was a month of preparation. The 8th Army was re-equipped and re-organised. Early in the month Churchill[6] had visited the troops in Egypt. He said that they were cheerful but couldn't understand why they had been repeatedly robbed of victory. It was imperative, at this stage, that Rommel should be prevented from reaching the Nile.

The Alam Halfa Ridge was one of the most important keys in the whole of the Allies' defence. So long as it was in British hands, Rommel's movement was restricted.

On 31 August, three days after Ray's last letter, Rommel attempted to break through the El Alamein line for a second time. The battle raged until 7 September, resulting in the enemy withdrawing. This was an extremely important victory. Much damage was caused to the Germans and Italians and it proved that the British tanks and infantry were a match for their enemies. Morale rose accordingly. It was just after this period of heightened confidence that the next letter was written:

16.9.42.

My dear Doreen,

A few more lines once again. Well, I am back in my old job in the squadron on the defence section. I have not received any mail from anyone for this last fortnight. I suppose it has been held up again.

The weather has gone a bit cooler again but we are now infested by millions of flies. These seem to get everywhere, in your eyes, mouth, nose and, worse still, in the food, however, we

6 Ray once told the anecdote of one of the Desert Rats whispering when he saw Churchill's victory sign, 'Do those two fingers mean two more years in this b— desert?'

manage to curb them a bit with numerous fly traps. The food we are getting is not too bad really but I think we are all just a little war weary and I expect you all are at home ... I shall be glad when I can get back to a job again and start building for the future otherwise I can see myself wandering around a middle aged man if this war keeps on much longer. Well dear I do hope you are taking care of yourself and keeping your chin up ...

Yours always,

Ray. x x x x x x

There is just one airgram from before the next critical Battle of Alamein commenced on 23 October. It mentions a letter from Max Miller.

12.10.42.

My dear Doreen,

... By the way Maxie Miller wrote to me last week and sent me some jokes etc., decent of him wasn't it?

Fondest love and kisses,

Ray x x x x x x

Max Miller wrote to Ray twice. One letter reads:

160, Marine Parade,
Brighton 7,
Sussex.

Aug. 7th 1942.

Dear Corporal Harris,

... I am enclosing you some material which I hope you will find useful. I can imagine how difficult it is for you to find new stuff out there ...

I shall be very interested to know if you receive this alright as I send out a tremendous amount of material and very seldom have replies. Remember me to any of the 'boys' out there who know me and tell them we are thinking of them and wishing them all a safe return.

Best Wishes,

Max Miller.

One of Ray's specialities with the concert party was impersonations of Max Miller.

Photograph of Max Miller courtesy of the Evening Argus.

There is now a gap in the correspondence.

After the Battle of Alam Halfa, the 8th Army had been very much strengthened by extra men and more than a thousand tanks. Amongst them were the new American Shermans. Over August and September, Rommel in the northern sector had built up defences with extensive minefields and artillery. Montgomery, who had taken over command of the 8th Army in August, planned to trick Rommel into thinking that he would be attacked from the south using such devices as dummy tanks (developed by Jasper Maskelyne).

Max Miller

Reply to
160 Marine Parade,
Brighton, 7,
Sussex.

Aug 7th 1942.

Dear Corporal Harris,

Many thanks for your letter of July 23rd. I am enclosing you some material, which I hope you will find useful. I can imagine how difficult it is for you to find new stuff way out there, I find it hard enough even in England to keep getting new routines. I shall be very interested to know if you receive this alright, as I send out a tremendous amount of material, and very seldom have replies.

Remember me to any of the "boys" out there who know me, and tell them we are thinking of them , and iwshing them all a safe return.

Best wishes,

Yours sincerely.

Max Miller.

7911536 L/CPL HARRIS R.A.J.
"JERBOA STROLLER'S " CONCERT PARTY.
C/O 152(ALBASSIA) LEAVE AND TRANSIT CAMP.
MIDDLE EAST FORCES.

One of Max Miller's letters to Ray, 7 August 1942.

In reality the main onslaught would be launched in the north. Corridors would have to be opened into the minefields.

Ray would have been placed in the south (opposite two enemy armoured divisions, 21st Panzer and Italian Ariete). Later he was moved up to the north to spearhead the breakout.

Ray prepared for battle on the 23 October and action commenced at 9.40 p.m. Later reports described a long procession of hundreds of guns, tanks and vehicles, all marching forward through choking dust and smoke and the relentless long-range, medium and heavy artillery fire. Between 23 October and 5 November, Ray fought in the Battle of Alamein, one of the most famous battles of all time. Despite all obstacles, poor visibility and relentless bombardment, Montgomery's plan worked. The remarkable victory became the turning point in the war. By 5 November, Rommel retreated realising that he had lost.

From this point the 8th Army began a 2,000-mile pursuit of the enemy across the desert. It moved in fighting formation and, as the tanks travelled forwards, there was fierce conflict between tanks and guns. The chase lasted six months, reaching Tunis on 7 May 1943.

By 12 November 1942 Ray had arrived at Tobruk. On 17 November (two days before the Division reached Benghazi), Ray sent an airgraph to Doreen.

17.11.42.

My dear Doreen,
Thanks a lot for your letters (containing programme and airgraph dated 18.10.42.). I have already posted an Army Xmas card to you and your mum and dad. I'm sorry that it is only the one card to you all but we are only allowed a limited number and it is impossible to buy anything else where I am at the moment. Anyway I know you will understand. I am looking forward to the photo.

I think I have had all your letters dear and also many thanks for the cutting about the 'Strollers'. Have you received that present I sent you? I hope it's not lost. I haven't been able to write regularly lately owing to the situation out here but will do my best to write as often as I can. Must close once again. With fondest love & kisses – regards to your mum and dad.

Yours, Ray. x x x x x x

On the 23 November they reached Agedabia. Another airgraph dated 28 November reads:

28.11.42.

My dear Doreen,

... Well things have started once again out here. I haven't had a moment to write a long letter so please don't get worried if you don't hear from me regularly ...

Yours,

Ray. x x x x x x

Chapter 4

Engagement

Before he reached Agheila on the 17 December 1942, Ray wrote on the 9 December proposing that he and Doreen should become engaged.

9.12.42.

My dear Doreen,

... Yes, things are going nicely out here at the moment and I hope they will continue to do so. The songs you mentioned in your letter are entirely new to me. I expect they will become popular out here around 1950, only I don't want to be here when they are. Yes darling, I am looking forward to us being all together again. What a party that's going to be eh? By the way dear, have your mum and dad any objections about you and I writing to one another? I hope not. Personally, I wish we were engaged don't you darling? I wonder if it would be possible. I could send a ring if I knew what size you take.

I know Vera would like to see us engaged and I think everybody would be happy about it don't you? Actually darling, we should have got together years ago. I wonder why we didn't. I always looked upon you dear as a friend of Vera, always coming in as I was going out or vice versa. Your letters have made me realize how sincere you are darling and how I love you. Do you really feel the same about it all? I do hope so darling. Anyway I would like to be engaged now and get married when I get back. After all I have a job to go back to and it would not cost a great deal of

(2)

they will continue to do so.
The songs you mentioned in your
letter are entirely new to me.
I expect they will become popular
out here round 1950 only I don't
want to be here when they are.
Yes, darling, I am looking forward
to us being all together again
what a party thats going to
be eh? By the way dear, have
your mum + dad any objections
about you + I writing to one
another. I hope not. Personally,
I wish we were engaged don't
you darling? I wonder if it
would be possible. I could send
a ring if I knew what size
you take. I know Vera would
like to see us engaged + I think
everybody would be happy about
it don't you? Actually darling,

Ray proposes to Doreen that they should be engaged.

money. Please let me know darling what you think. Must close now. With fondest love and kisses. Please write soon.

Yours always,
Ray. x x x x x x

A Christmas card follows printed:

So far and yet so near in our hearts as we wish you a Merry Christmas
Greetings from the Middle East.

Ray writes:

To Doreen, Mr. & Mrs. Sellman with love and kindest regards, and hoping for a re-union in the very near future.

Ray's Christmas card sent 1943.

Around this time, planning started for the advance on Tripoli. Ray's division was to take a route inland across country. Before they reached Buerat, on the 15 January 1942, Ray replied to Doreen's airgraph dated 13 December 1942. There is no mention of whether she has accepted his proposal but, as his letter states, he was still waiting for some of her letters to arrive.

10.1.43.

My dear Doreen,

Many thanks for airgraph dated 13.12.42. received today. I certainly wish that I could have spent Xmas with you all at dear old Brighton, but never mind, I am looking forward to some good times in the future.

Prior to your last airgraph today I have not heard from you for some time but expect all your mail will arrive in due course ...

Yours always,
Ray. x x x x x x

On 19 January 1943, Tarhuna was reached. On 22 January 1943 there was a great deal of excitement as the capture of Tripoli (the next day) was anticipated. Under a full moon they entered the city on the 23 January. In the morning, there was jubilation when the inhabitants realised that the troops were British.

Up to the end of January the 65-mile advance from Tripoli was fraught with danger. There were many mines and booby-traps, and bridges had been destroyed.

On 10 February Ray wrote to Doreen.

10.2.43.

My dear Doreen,

... I'm so sorry I haven't been able to write for a week or so but I have been so busy one way and another. I have been asked to produce a concert for the 'lads' and have written out an entirely

new show which will last round about two hours, so you can guess I have been fully occupied getting all the sketches, scripts and materials together.

Anyway, you know dear that, even if I cannot write as often as I would like to, I am always thinking of you ...

Yours always,

Ray. x x x x x x

On 16 February they entered Medenine and Ray's next letter reveals that Doreen has accepted his proposal.

23.2.43.

My dear Doreen,

Just a few lines in answer to your airmail lettercard received today. I have already received a letter from Dad with congratulations and I'm so pleased that everybody feels the same way about us. I know everything is going to be O.K. and am counting the days until I am saying 'hello!' again. I am very busy at the moment producing a show for the 'lads' of the squadron and I think it's going to turn out O.K. Please give mum and dad my fondest regards dear and tell them I'm looking forward to a letter. Must close now with fondest love and kisses. Please write again soon.

Yours always,

Ray. x x x x x x

By early March, it was clear that Rommel, by now a very sick man, had decided that unless his troops attacked, the British would be successful in driving them from Africa. British dummy tanks tricked the enemy into an area where it came under fire. There was a tank battle known as the Battle of Medenine but British casualties were light.

More heavy losses were suffered by the Germans and Italians when Montgomery attacked the Mareth Line on 16 March.

From 18 to the 30 March, the Division wasn't involved in much fighting. It was during this period that Ray wrote his next letters.

23.3.43.

My dear Doreen,
Many thanks for your airgraphs received this week. I was so pleased to hear that you are all keeping O.K. dear. I had a letter from your Dad so am writing back to him. Now about the ring dear. I think it would be better after all, to leave it until I get back as you suggest.

I am a bit dubious about sending anything else from this country, after the other present being lost. I am annoyed about that, still it's just bad luck I suppose, anyway I wouldn't like anything else to go the same way. Things are pretty well the same here at the moment but we are all hoping for a speedy conclusion. I think I mentioned in my previous letter darling, that I was producing a show for the 'lads'. We presented it to the squadron on 15th March (last Monday) and it went over very well. Since then, we have been very busy giving shows to other units nearby who have welcomed us with open arms, as there is very little entertainment up here except for a travelling cinema from time to time ... don't forget that if you don't hear from me for some weeks please don't worry. I will write as often as I possibly can ...

Yours always,
Ray. x x x x x x

30.3.43.

My dear Doreen,
Just a few lines to wish you many happy returns of your birthday. I'm sorry I can't manage to get even a card where I am at the moment but I know you will understand dear. I hope that I shall be home for your next one, so we can celebrate in real style. No more news this time so will close with love and kisses, hoping to

hear from you again soon,
Yours,
Ray. x x x x x x

By the time April arrived there was a steady advance, and on 30 April the 7th Armoured Division transferred to the 1st Army. There is one letter written in April.

15.4.43.

My dear Doreen,
Many thanks for your letters and airgraph which I was so pleased to receive. I'm pleased to say that we are expecting to be quite busy with the concert party very soon now. At the moment we are polishing up the show. There are twelve of us altogether and, although it is not dressed so well as the original 'Strollers', we don't do too badly. We have given it the title 'Rats to the Blue' ('Blue' being as you probably know slang for desert) and seeing that the 7th Armoured Division are the original 'Desert Rats', the title is quite appropriate. I heard from Vera the other day and she tells me that they went to see 'Desert Victory' and thoroughly enjoyed it. I wouldn't mind seeing it myself. She mentions that there are still a number of men still being posted abroad. I do hope Eddie doesn't have to go.

Yes! I'm looking forward to being all together again in Brighton, we certainly will have to make up for lost time, won't we dear? I hope it won't be long now. I suppose 'Sherry's' is still going strong, although I expect the old gang has gone, never mind I'll bet they will all be back again one day. I wish I were back in England to start making a few plans, it's all so very difficult out here and you can do nothing. Dad seems to be doing very well in his present business and they are expecting to move to a flat above the shop. Well darling there's not much more news this time so I will close with fondest love and kisses to you and fondest regards to your mum and dad.
Hoping to hear from you soon,
Ray. x x x x x x

By 2 May Ray's division had arrived at El Krib, 40 miles west of Tunis. On 7 May 1943 Tunis was entered. Cheering crowds greeted the victorious British troops.

The campaign that had started six months ago at El Alamein ended. Chasing the German army, 2,000 miles had been travelled in 180 days. Victory was now complete.

Ray's next letter tells Doreen the African campaign is over.

18.5.43.

My dear Doreen,

I'm so sorry dear that I haven't been able to write for so long, but as you know things have been moving so quickly out here that I haven't really been able to settle down. Well! The African campaign seems to have come to a close at last and the general topic is 'what now?' Of course, rumours are rife at the moment, but nobody really knows what is going to happen and it is no good taking any notice of the yarns that are spreading around, so the only thing to do is to wait and see. Please thank your mum for her very welcome letter, it was nice of her to write. Tell her I am writing back.

I am so pleased to hear that your dad is doing so well with his show and I hope that business continues to be good. We have just finished a busy four days with the concert party giving two shows a day in some cases, and, as all our performances are given in the open air, you can guess it's pretty hot work for the lads, with an African sun beating down on them. We also expect to be pretty busy during the next few weeks as everybody will probably be static and the most important thing is to keep the 'boys' and the units entertained. I've got to produce a new show soon but Lord knows where the material is coming from, it's all pretty difficult out here, still I suppose I'll get by O.K. Well darling, I do hope that you are taking care of yourself and not working too hard. Please give your mum and dad my fondest regards, anyway I shall be writing to them.

Must close now with fondest love and kisses. Please write again soon.

Yours always,

Ray. x x x x x x

The 7th Arm'd Div. was moved to Bou Arada, 50 miles southwest of Tunis. There was a general feeling of disappointment as they had hoped to be nearer civilisation. This was followed by a move to Homs, 60 miles east of Tripoli on the coast, and there were then three months to prepare for the next campaign in Italy. The Jerboa Club was set up, containing a cinema and theatre for ENSA[7] and the other concert parties (one being Ray's 'Jerboa Strollers'). A great deal of football was played and there was much bathing in the sea.

The next batch of letters is mainly concerned with the announcement of Ray and Doreen's engagement and concert parties.

The letter dated 30 May 1943 mentions that Doreen has bought the ring.

30.5.43.

My own darling,

Many thanks for your letters, airgraphs and W.F.[8] I am so pleased you have managed to get the ring and if you will let me know the cost I will forward the cash. I am up to my neck in work at the moment dear, with an entirely new show which I am presenting on 2nd June. We have managed to procure an old Roman amphitheatre which has been converted. It can seat about 7,000 people so you can guess it's a big affair and the show has got to be good. I do hope your Dad can manage to get our engagement announced in the W.F. I think Vera has still got the old photo of me.

Please let me have a cutting if it does appear won't you?

7 ENSA – Entertainments National Service Association, set up in 1939 as an organisation to entertain the troops

8 World's Fair

Turning the subject to songs I haven't heard many of those you mention darling.

I am featuring a few old favourites in the new show such as: 'Rain in the Sky', 'The Last All Clear', 'I'll Think of You', 'Maybe', 'I Want to Go Back in the Evening', 'Kiss the Boys Goodbye' and a few others. All of them pretty old, but still popular with the 'lads'. We are presenting the show once nightly at 6 p.m. for 3 nights and a matinée on the last day. I do wish you could be there darling although some of the sketches and gags are hardly for female ears, but then we have to cater for everybody. Well darling I shall have to close once again with fondest love and kisses and please give mum and dad my fondest regards.

Please write again soon.

Yours always,

Ray x x x x x x

18.6.43.

My own darling,

I have just sent you a cable to let you know I have received all your mail. I haven't been able to write a line for the last ten days. I have just returned from a tour with the show and what a tour, nineteen shows in ten days, each one lasting two hours! We have played to over 30,000 people in that time so you can guess what time I've had to call my own. I received another W.F. yesterday. Thanks a lot darling! By the way, I'm so pleased about the announcement dear. I think perhaps it would be best if you could enclose the cutting in a letter and not send the whole paper, as a letter would reach me much more quickly and an ordinary newspaper coming by boat mail stands a good chance of getting lost and I wouldn't like that to happen, so would you cut it out and enclose it in a letter darling?

Yes I would like some Brighton papers dear if you could send some on, they would make interesting reading. There's not much news this time except that I go into rehearsals for a new show tomorrow, so shall be busy again. I heard from Vera today from the new address. It sounds a nice place and I am looking forward to seeing it. Well darling, many thanks for all your letters and I will write as often as I can. Must close now with fondest love and kisses and best wishes to mum and dad. Please write again soon.

Yours always,
Ray. x x x x x x

A telegram dated 19 June 1943 is possibly the one mentioned in the last letter:

VERY HAPPY TO HEAR FROM YOU DEAREST. AM FIT AND WELL. WRITING. FONDEST LOVE DARLING.

3.7.43.

My own darling,
Have just received your letter containing the photo of yourself. Well darling I think it's charming and certainly the best I have seen of you. What a lovely hair style you are wearing dear, it does suit you. I am so pleased with it and shall keep it with me always.

Yes! Vera has written and told me all about the new house and of course I am looking forward to seeing it. By the way darling you have never said how much the ring cost. Please let me know and I will forward the cash on. I do hope it won't be long now darling before I am back with you and we can start making plans for the future. Anyway I do think there is nothing to stop us from getting married right away, after all, we have got a few years to make up for haven't we darling? I do hope you won't get tired of waiting for me dear.

I know it's a long, long time for us both but it will be worth waiting for won't it darling? You know darling I shall always love you and am counting the days until I am holding you in my arms and saying hello! Well my sweet I shall have to close once again with all my love and kisses and fondest regards to mum

and dad. Please write again soon.
Yours always and always,
Your loving fiancé,
Ray. x x x x x x

19.7.43.

My own darling,
Many thanks for your airmail lettercards and the W.F. (dated 15th May), so you can guess how long it takes for a newspaper to arrive. Anyway I am looking forward to the one with our engagement in, and I hope it won't get lost. The words of 'All Our Tomorrows' are certainly great darling. Is the tune as good? If so I shall have to put it in the show.

We had the big E.N.S.A. Show 'Springtime' out here not long ago. The cast included Leslie Henson and Vivien Leigh (who looked beautiful but that's about all) and Beatrice Lille who stole the show. Fairly good entertainment for about two hours but nothing sensational. I'm so pleased to hear that your Dad is doing so well with the show and I hope business keeps up for him. I wonder how long it really will be before I am back, but as you say dear, one day gone is one day nearer ...
Yours always,
Ray. x x x x x x

24.7.43.

My own darling,
Many thanks for your A.M. letter card dated 12/7/43. Now darling, I am making arrangements to send some money home for Dad and Vera to keep for me.

This will take a couple of months or so, but when it does arrive I have asked Dad to send £4 on to you and that will cover the cost of the ring and also leave a little over with which you can buy something for yourself darling. I hope you have a nice time at Brighton this year and I wish I was there to spend it with you darling ...

Yours always,
Ray. x x x x x x

31.7.43.

My own darling,
Many thanks for your A.M. letter card dated 17.7.43. Yes! The show has been running O.K. up to now. Last night we gave a performance at a large hospital nearby and everything went over really big. It may be, however, our last show for some time, as today we have to return to our squadron for duty. I am trying to get the whole show into E.N.S.A. but don't know whether I shall be successful or not.

It seems such a pity to break up such a good show as we have at the present time ... As you say dear, we really can't make many plans for the future, but I am saving up as much money as I can and should come out of the army with enough to give us a start. Well dear, I think the words of 'Constancy' are very nice indeed and that's the way I feel too ...

Yours always,
Ray. x x x x x x

The announcement of Ray and Doreen's engagement in the World's Fair (which Ray was to receive on 20 August) read:

The engagement is announced of L/Cpl. Ray Harris, son of Mr. F.C. Harris, and Miss Doreen Margaret Sellman, daughter of Mr. & Mrs. A. Sellman. L/Cpl Harris is at present serving in the Middle East and is attached to the 'Rats of the Blue' Concert Party of which he is principal comedian and producer. Miss Sellman is the only daughter of our contributor 'Southdown'.

R. Garigliano
R. Agnena
R. Volturno
R. Sarno
GULF OF NAPLES
GULF OF SALERNO

1. Cicola
2. Mt Massico
3. Mondragone
4. Aversa
5. Capua
6. Cardito
7. Naples
8. Mt Vesuvius
9. Pompeii
10. Scafati
11. Salerno
12. Sorrento

Sketch map of S. Italy

Chapter 5

ITALY

At the end of July 1943 Ray, as stated in the previous letter, was recalled to duty in preparation for the invasion of Italy. There had been a visit from the King (not mentioned by Ray as he was probably on tour at the time). There had also been training in landing on a hostile shore and practice in fighting in terrain differing greatly from the desert.

The invasion of Sicily (not involving the 7th Arm'd Div.) started on 10 July and was completed by 16 August. At the beginning of August Ray's division started to equip itself again. His old tank would be replaced with a new one. It would also have to be waterproofed for driving in up to six feet of water. By 27 August the tanks were packed with rations and they were ready to go.

The letters Ray wrote during these final preparations mention nothing of the preparations themselves. Their somewhat repetitious flavour at this period shows how little he could reveal. All topics already included in previous letters have been omitted.

8.8.43.

My dearest one,

... Things are very quiet here now, just the usual routine in fact. I am on guard tonight ...

Yours always and always,

Ray. x x x x x x

21.8.43.

My own darling,

Just a few lines to say that the W.F. with the engagement photos arrived yesterday. I think they are both very good don't you dear? ... I shall be glad to get back [to Brighton].

I suppose the big problem will be getting a decent job. Of course I can always get back to Lawsons,[9] *well I shall have to see, I suppose.*

I am saving a few pounds for the future darling, as we shall need them and things are bound to be very expensive, anyway once we are started I know we shall be O.K. dear ...

Yours always,

Ray. x x x x x x

27.8.43.

My own darling,

... I bet the play 'No Orchids for Miss Blandish' was good wasn't it darling? I have read the book (who hasn't?) and what a book! I should imagine the old Hippodrome was packed every night wasn't it? I can almost see the men (during certain scenes of the play, if it's anything like the book), coughing and reaching for their cigarette cases and their girlfriends blushing and suddenly finding the adverts on the programme very interesting.

Shades of Maxie Miller, remember darling? Well darling, don't forget to write and tell me more about the play next time ...

Yours always,

Ray. x x x x x x

6.9.43.

My dearest one,

... I'm afraid I haven't much news this time except that I am keeping fit and well and still counting the days until I see you again. I have

9 Store at 21 Gloucester Place, Brighton

just been wondering how much money we shall need when I get back and I do hope darling that we won't have to resort to saving up for years. That takes too long doesn't it?

Yours always and always,

Ray. x x x x x x

The next letter bears a different address which confirms that Ray had already landed in Italy.

This operation was the opening of the second front in Europe. From Tripoli Ray's division was taken by ship to Salerno, south of Naples. As they sailed on 8 September they heard General Eisenhower's broadcast that Italy had surrendered, but the Germans were quick to take over from the Italians. For the first time, the 7th Arm'd Div. was part of the American army. The plan (called Operation Avalanche) was for the 46th and 56th Infantry Divisions to attack in the Bay of Salerno and then the 7th Arm'd Div. would break out of the bridgehead afterwards. Although there was continuous enemy assault, by 27 September, after a fierce struggle (and helped by the 8th Army's landing at the 'toe' of Italy), the Division was ready to break out of the bridgehead formed by the Americans with the 23rd Armoured Brigade under command.

The first destination was Scafati on the River Sarno and then the 23rd Division would drive straight on to Naples, whilst the rest travelled north of Vesuvius heading for Capua on the River Volturno.

Travelling through Italy was no easy task. Many roads had to be repaired and, in the marshy areas, there was the danger of malaria. All the villages and towns gave the Allies a warm welcome and a priest at Scafati sprinkled the armoured cars with holy water.

The first letter Ray wrote from Italy is undated.

7911536 L/CPL Harris R.A.J.,
H.Q. Squadron 7th Armoured Div.,
C.M.F.

My dearest one,
Many thanks for your A.M. lettercard dated [9.9.43.] *... Well darling, I can't tell you a lot of news this time as the censorship is still very strict, anyway, please don't forget my new address at the top of the letter card will you dear?*

I expect you will be glad when your Dad gets back from his tour darling. Please give him my fondest regards and best wishes won't you?

By the way, how's the chances of some more photos darling? ... It shakes me sometimes dear when I open my pay-book and read 'age on enlistment 26' and here I am nearly thirty, still I am keeping fit and well which is the main thing I suppose. It is still pretty hot and we all keep our suntan, in fact none of us seem to have lost it in nearly three years. I should have liked to have been with you at the 'No Orchids' play darling. Anyway, get the book if you get the chance. It's pretty good, well for broad minded people anyway. If you are easily shocked don't read it. Well darling I must close once again with fondest love and kisses.

Please write again soon,
Yours always,
Ray. x x x x x x

On 3 October progress was delayed by opposition at Cardito, the enemy hidden in vineyards and standing maize, but Cardito was captured and it was regarded as the Allies' most successful battle in Italy. On 5 October (Ray's birthday) the tanks made a causeway to enable crossing over a large drainage dyke called Regi Lagni. There was then an advance towards the Volturno. This was crossed between 7 and 16 October. A large bank was dug and a bulldozer employed to help the tanks across.

Throughout the advance the Division had met with very tough conditions, both from fierce resistance from the enemy and from the difficulty of navigating close countryside, narrow roads, demolitions and deep mud all exacerbated by bad weather. By 22 October they were ready to meet the enemy at the River Garigliano. During this period Ray revealed to Doreen his whereabouts.

(2)
forward to one.
Well, the weather here in Italy is
certanly more like the English
climate, & a welcome relief from
the desert.
We are getting bags of apples,
fresh potatoes, & nuts, quite a
novelty for us.
It is a beautiful country & the
people are very friendly, although
we are experiencing a little
difficulty with the language.
Well darling, there is no need
for me to say how I am yearning
to be home again with you,
& I do hope it won't be long
now. I heard from Dad yesterday
telling me he had received the
money I sent. They all seem to

One of Ray's letters from Italy (14.10.1943).

10.10.43.

My dearest one,

Just a few lines to let you know I'm keeping O.K. I expect you have received my new address by now haven't you darling? I can't tell you a great deal of news but I am able to say that we are now in Italy. I suppose you probably guessed that dear ...

I may be able to buy a few things in this country. Is there anything special you want dear? I can probably get hold of some stockings. Let me know will you? And I will send you and Vera some on. Must close now with all my love and kisses.

Yours always,

Ray. x x x x x x

14.10.43.

My dearest one,

... Well the weather here in Italy is certainly more like the English climate and a welcome relief from the desert.

We are getting bags of apples, fresh potatoes and nuts, quite a novelty for us. It is a beautiful country and the people are very friendly, although we are experiencing a little difficulty with the language. Well darling there is no need for me to say how I am yearning to be home again with you, and I do hope it won't be long now ... Peter[10] *appears to be getting quite a big boy now and I am certainly looking forward to seeing him. By the way darling, many thanks for Rex's address. I am writing to him today. He appears (by his address) to have moved back to his mother's place. It's quite a nice flat,*[11] *what I can remember of it. Well darling, news is scarce this time, so I will close with all my love and kisses, hoping to hear from you again soon.*

Yours always,

Ray. x x x x x x

---

10 Vera and Eddie's son

11 In Albert Road, Brighton, where Ray and Doreen would eventually live

22.10.43.

My own darling,

... Please don't bother to send a Christmas present darling as you can't really depend on it arriving safely, however, I am looking forward to the photos you mention and I shall be more than satisfied with them as a present when they arrive dear ...

The W.F.'s are especially acceptable, as, after I have read them, I pass them on to a pal of mine (who is in the show business in civvie street) and we both are always looking forward to them... Yes darling, it certainly is some time since we saw one another last and I do hope we shan't find a big difference in each other ...

Yours always,
Ray. x x x x x x

31.10.43.

My own darling,

... Unfortunately out here there are no decent photographers, so I don't know when I shall be able to get some done again. However, I did get one done by a street photographer but it wasn't very good. I sent it to Vera, if you would like it darling, just write and ask for it ...

I was surprised and inwardly pleased that you saw Donald Peers in a film. What was the name of the picture darling? I certainly would like to see it myself. I wonder how many of his records are left at home, I expect I shall have to start another collection when I get back ... Well my darling, space is short, so I will close once again with all my love and kisses ...

Yours always,
Ray. x x x x x x

P.S. You are always in my thoughts darling and I'm counting the days.

Ray (on left) on leave at Pompeii, 1943.

The enemy continued to destroy every bridge as it withdrew and the Allies advanced towards the Agnena River near the coast. They went via Capua, the bridge of which could only bear single tanks. The enemy continued to attack but on 1 November Mondragone and the ridge on Monte Massico were taken. There was another struggle at Cicola but again the Division's tanks were victorious and, after reaching the River Garigliano the Division withdrew behind Massico. On 7 November all withdrew to Aversa and the vehicles were handed to the 5th Canadian Armoured Division. A few days later they moved to the Sorrento Peninsula from which there was some local leave but the weather was very poor. There is a photograph of Ray in Pompeii revealing that his leave was taken there.

15.11.43.

My own darling,
... Many thanks for the cigarettes darling, they will make a very acceptable Xmas present ...

Well darling, there's not much news this time, as everything is very quiet but you know darling I am always thinking of you and counting the time until I see you again. I'm afraid Xmas cards are pretty scarce again this year, so it will have to be another Army issue once more, anyway I know you will understand darling ...

Yours always and always,
Ray. x x x x x x

A day later Ray writes again.

16.11.43.

My own darling,
... Well darling, there's no need for me to tell you that I am always thinking of you and I feel sure that it won't be long before the war is over. I fully expect 1944 to be victory year, and then we both can start planning for our future ... He's [Rex] *all for being best man on our big day but I expect Eddie will want that job ...*

Yes I remember you at 15 when Rex and I used to stroll into the shop for the inevitable 3d Players round about Thurs. when funds were low. The years certainly roll on don't they darling? They were happy days but I think we both have happier days ahead of us. It is always a great comfort to me to know that you have waited so patiently for me darling and that I have you to come home to ...

Yours always and always,
Ray. x x x x x x

2.12.43.

My own darling,
... The weather has turned bitterly cold and the old top coats and gloves are very much in use. It's funny to see oranges growing out here with the weather so cold, but it does not seem to make any difference to them and there are plenty. I wish I could send some home.

By the way, I managed to get some stockings (only three pairs though) also some powder, lipstick and face cream so I shall be sending them on to you dear ...

Yours always,
Ray. x x x x x x

In December 1943 most of the Division drove through Naples with cheering crowds waving. On 20 December they embarked at Naples' dock after queueing for most of the day. Christmas was spent at sea. A daily Routine Orders sheet written by Lt Colonel HRH Rouquette MCRA (officer commanding troops on board) bears the notice that on Christmas Day '*[at] 2000 hours in the Cinema there will be, A Christmas Day Review – "Homeward Bound" designed for broadcasting. The company includes several old favourites from the "Jerboa Strollers"*'.

Chapter 6

Home and Marriage

On 7 January 1944, Ray arrived with his division at Glasgow and from there travelled by train to Brandon, Norfolk. A standard postcard was sent to Doreen:

> *Have arrived home safe and well. Letters addressed as below will reach me, but I will be coming on leave shortly.*
>
> *From Ray/ H.Q. Squadron, 7th Armoured Div., A.P.O, No. 5990.*

Brandon was not an attractive place. It was a bleak, sandy wasteland interspersed with dilapidated Nissen huts and tall pine trees. Conditions were far from ideal. There was less food than there had been abroad, with centralised cooking, small fuel allowances and leave problems.

Before Britain and America could launch a final invasion of Europe, they had to win command of the air over the Channel and the invasion area in France. They had to find a way to hold back the German troops while they landed their own armies and equipment.

When the Division arrived, however, its leave was long overdue, so before preparations for D-Day started, Doreen received a telegram from Brighton:

> *ARRIVED SAFELY YESTERDAY. WRITING. LOVE RAY.*

Then, on 13 January, the message that Doreen had been waiting for:

HOME ON LEAVE. CAN YOU COME DOWN? RAY.

The next letter is dated 4 February 1944 and the success of Doreen and Ray's reunion is shown in Ray's single-minded determination to get married in his next letter.

4.2.44.

My own darling,

Well here I am back again worse luck. All my pals seem to have arrived back <u>married</u> and seemed quite surprised that I am still single. Now darling, I think we definitely will get married on my next leave, which will be ten days. I can get this on either Feb. 10th, Feb. 17th or Feb. 24th.

Of course they can't guarantee anything, but are going to do their best and try and get us the date we want. Now darling, which date shall I try and get? I think perhaps we had better make it the registry office darling, as ten days is not a lot of time to get married in. Anyway, looking at everything from a practical point of view, I think it's best after all darling. The main thing is we shall be married shan't we? Another thing is the money point of view. As you know I have only £50 dear and I think a church wedding would make a nasty hole in that.

The honeymoon is the main thing and that's where the money should go ... There is no need for me to say how much I miss you darling and am counting the hours until our wedding day ...

All my love darling,
Ray. x x x x x x

10.2.44.

My own darling,

I was so pleased to receive your letter today. Well darling, I have been making a few enquiries among the lads who have just got married and it seems that we shall be able to get a special licence for £2.2.0., so that's not too bad is it darling? Yes! I think we may as well make it a church wedding after all dear, it shouldn't cost a lot. Now darling, I will try my best to get leave on the 24th (I think it will be pretty certain if I tell them I'm getting married).

The only thing is that I shan't be able to get my pass until 6 o'clock in the evening on the Thurs., so I shan't be able to get away until late at night. This means that I shan't get home until the hours of Friday morning (25th). The whole trouble is darling, that I shan't have a lot of time to make arrangements for the wedding.

I don't want to spend nearly all of my ten days leave getting things ready and only having about two days with you darling. You understand what I mean don't you dear? I was wondering whether you could manage to get down a day or two earlier and get a few things ready so that we don't lose too much time? Anyway please let me know, won't you darling. There's no need for me to tell you dear that I am counting the hours until I see you again. You know how much I love you darling and I know we shall both be very happy ...

I think we will get away to somewhere very quiet for the honeymoon don't you darling? Or would you rather go up to London? ...

Yours for always and always,
Ray. x x x x x x

12.2.44.

My own darling,
Many thanks for your two letters received O.K. I am so pleased to hear that Dad and Mum can manage to get down a little early. It is very good of them indeed and will save us a little time. Please thank them for me darling. Dad will advance them what money they require, as my money is in his banking account and can be drawn at any time. Please don't forget to tell them about this,

will you darling? Yes! I have heard about the cheap rates for the services re the licence. It will be a great help won't it dear?

I think the 24th is pretty certain dear and we can practically say it will be O.K. I will write to Rex later on.

I wrote to Eddie to ask him if he can alter his leave date to the 25th as I did want him to be best man. I do hope he can manage it. I hope everything works out O.K., especially as regards the catering. It will certainly take a load off my mind if Mum and Dad can handle this. Well darling, I think that's all for now. I will write again in a day or two. Please write and let me know how things are going won't you dear? All my love darling to yourself and Mum and Dad.

Yours always,
Ray. x x x x x x

17.2.44.

My own darling,
... I haven't heard from you for six days now, I expect the mail's held up again. Montgomery inspected us today, quite a long parade of course. Rumour has it that the King is coming down next Thursday.

Now, if he does, I may not be able to get my leave pass until Thursday afternoon, which will mean that I shan't get to Brighton until pretty late Thursday night. Anyway darling, I will let you know directly I know for sure. Well darling, there's not much more except that I am counting the hours until the 26th. We shall have to nip round pretty quickly on the Friday getting the ring and making last minute arrangements shan't we darling? Please let me know how things are going won't you dear? I must close now darling with all my love and kisses.

Yours always,
Ray. x x x x x x

18.2.44.

My own darling,
Many thanks for letter dated [Feb. 15] *received today. I have just seen my Sergeant Major and he assured me that I will get my leave on the 24th, so we can take it as definite darling.*

I think it is a good idea for you to get the ring dear as soon as possible. As you say darling, it will save a bit of time, so will you do that?

Well darling, about the honeymoon. Don't you think it will take a bit of time travelling to Salisbury? We do want to snatch every bit of time we can don't we darling? I was thinking that perhaps if we booked a decent hotel in Brighton it would be best after all. Brighton is very near and dear to both of us and there are always shows and amusements for us to go to. We can get to a hotel in a nice quiet part of the town, Hove, perhaps. It would save a lot of rushing off at the last moment too. What do you think darling?

Anyway, we will talk it over, when I see you, as you won't get this letter until Tues., or Wed. Well darling, I hope you receive the telegram I am sending tomorrow (Sat.) O.K. Must close now with all my love and kisses until Thursday.

Yours always,
Ray. x x x x x x

19.2.44.

HOME ON THURSDAY. LOVE RAY.

19.2.44.

My own darling,
Many thanks for letter received. Well first of all I'll answer your questions.

Born 5th Oct. 1913 at Croughton, Northants. Surname, Harris. Christian names, Albert John. Occupation on joining army, Salesman. Religion, Church of England.

Well darling that's the lot. If there should be any more Vera will be able to tell you. I'm so glad that things are going O.K., and everybody seems so kind and willing to help. It's certainly taken a load off my mind.

I wrote you a letter yesterday, addressed to 4, St. Andrews Road,[12] *saying that I think round about Brighton will be best for the honeymoon and I'm glad you agree darling.*

Well dear, I'm on guard in ten minutes time (my last before my leave, thank goodness!), so I will close once again with all my love and kisses. In haste to catch the post.

Yours always and always,

Ray. x x x x x x

A surviving newspaper cutting describes the wedding which took place as planned on 26 February 1944.

A Brighton soldier, Lance Corporal Ray Harris of R.A.C. who has just returned home from Italy, was the bridegroom at a wedding which took place at St. Peter's Church Preston on Saturday, when the bride was Miss Margaret Doreen Sellman, daughter of Mr. and Mrs. A. Sellman.

... The Rev. R. M. Roper officiated. Given away by her father, the bride was attired in a grey coat and powder blue dress with burgundy accessories. She wore a spray of carnations and carried an ivory Prayer Book. The attendants were Mrs. J. Leppard and Miss. B. Knight (friends of the bride) and Miss. M. Patching (cousin of the bride). The two seniors wore brown costumes with sprays of carnations and the junior bridesmaid was dressed in turquoise blue and carried a posy of violets. Mr. B.R. Morrison (friend of the bridegroom) was best man.

12 Vera and Eddie's address

Doreen and Ray's wedding, 26th February 1944.

Chapter 7

Preparation for D-Day

Ray's next letter finds him back at Brandon.

7.3.44.

My own darling wife,

Just a few lines to let you know that I arrived yesterday round about 5 o'clock. Well darling, everything seems pretty miserable now as you can guess and the only thing I am interested in is some more leave ... I have heard tonight on very good authority that the 7th may be lucky enough to get another ten days. Well my darling there's no need for me to say how much I am missing you, but am trying to be as cheerful as possible in the hope it won't be long before I am with you again. I wonder how the old gang is at Milton Hall Hotel,[13] *still we didn't have a bad time did we darling?*

As you say, we have years of happiness in front of us. I saw my pay sergeant this morning and arranged for your allowance dear ... There's not really a lot of news from this lousy dump this time darling ... all of my love and kisses to you darling. Please write soon and God bless.

Your loving husband,

Ray. x x x x x x

Two days later Ray reveals that he is going to Yarmouth.

13 Hotel in Montpelier Road, Brighton, where Ray and Doreen spent their honeymoon

9.3.44

My own darling wife,

... Well darling I have just heard today that I am going to Yarmouth for a few weeks. I go tomorrow (Friday) with a sergeant and about six troopers.

As far as I can gather we are going to do staff jobs at a driving school, so shall be keeping out of trouble for a time.

Anyway it will make a change from this horrible place and I am lucky to be going ... I am missing you so much darling ... All my love and kisses and God bless.

Your loving husband,

Ray. x x x x x x

The next letter comes from Lowestoft.

7911536 L/CPL Harris R.,
Driving School,
C/o P.O. Lowestoft,
Suffolk.

My own darling wife,

Just a few lines to let you know my new address (which you see above). Whatever you do darling don't put on your envelope anything about H.Q. Squadron 7th Armoured Div., as this job we are on at the moment is something to do with security ... We arrived here yesterday and are just getting settled in.

It's not too bad really, about a mile from the town. I understand we shall be here for about six weeks on the permanent staff. Anyway, it's better than Brandon. Well, my darling there's no need for me to tell you how much I'm missing you and I'm praying it won't be long before I am holding you in my arms again. I feel sure it won't be long now before this racket is over and then we can start looking towards the future ... I certainly miss that double bed at Milton Hall don't you darling? I wonder how all the old folks are doing there, still talking about the gas mask inspection I bet ...I've been terribly busy lately darling and, to crown it all, I got detailed for guard tonight (Saturday of all nights). How I wish you and I were just strolling down Montpelier Rd., now don't you dear?

Still there are plenty of happy days ahead of us. Well my dearest one I shall have to close once again with love to Mum and Dad. So goodnight my darling and God Bless.

With all my love and kisses,

Your loving husband,

Ray. x x x x x x

P.S. Please write soon.

As Ray states in the previous letter, there were very strict security precautions in place all around Britain's coast during the invasion of France preparations. The Division had to be trained in new weapons and Cromwell tanks (all their old equipment had been left in Italy). The change of tank was controversial. It had a Rolls-Royce engine but many minor faults. However, it was fast and didn't burst into flames as quickly when hit as the Sherman tended to.

The Division had to prepare for assault landings in the face of opposition.

There were practice runs (with the navy) in the use of LSTs (Landing Ship Tanks), in landing on the beach or large rafts and in the waterproofing of vehicles (including tanks) as the landing would be wet. There were new recruits to the Division but many of the solders preparing were like Ray who had been fighting continuously since 1941.

In all the letters of this period, Ray was hoping to get back to England to Doreen, his new wife, but in fact, he was frustrated at every turn.

16.3.44.

My own darling,

... Well darling I'm getting on O.K. now but am really working <u>*hard*</u> *for a change and my spare time is really limited ...*

There's no definite news about more leave yet, perhaps later on, I hope. I am thinking of you always my darling. Still it won't be long now I know ...

All my love and kisses darling and God Bless.

Your loving husband,

Ray. x x x x x x

P.S. Please write again soon darling.

20.3.44.

My own darling wife,

... It is quite nice here in Lowestoft and, although we are working long hours, we do get a bit of time off. I'm hoping that this job will last a week or two as it is a lot better than Brandon. The wedding presents sound very nice darling. I shall have to see them when I come on leave.

I may be able to manage a long week-end to Cannock, that is from Friday to Monday but we have to pay our own train fare and I think it's pretty expensive. What do you think darling? Anyway I will see later on ...

Love and kisses to you darling.

Your loving husband,

Ray. x x x x x x

Thurs.

My own darling wife,

... I'm so pleased to hear that you have got the army pay book already darling. How much do they allow you as I understand it differs a bit according to what part of the country you live in ... We are still up to our necks in work, but tomorrow night, I am scrounging a couple of hours off, as I have entered for a talent competition at the local cinema, so wish me luck darling. The first prize is only £1 but it's better than nothing isn't it?

I think I stand a good chance anyway. Well darling, there are still rumours floating about re more leave, but nothing really official yet, anyway let's keep hoping. Tell Mum the cake was 'just the job' and it's all gone ...

I am counting the hours until I see you again. I'm hoping it will be soon now. By the way, I hope you received the birthday card O.K. It was the best I could get. I don't think anybody has birthdays round this way ... I love you and you are always in my thoughts my dearest ...

All my love and kisses to you darling and God Bless.

Your loving husband,

Ray. x x x x x x

P.S. Write again soon dear.

The next letter promises a definite leave date.

25.3.44.

My own darling wife,

... Well darling, your thoughts must have been with me at the talent competition last night. I won the first prize £1 pretty easily (although I was a bit off form according to my pals who all turned up to see the show). Anyway I had very little opposition except for a couple of quite good crooners and piano players. My act went down very well. Anyway the manager was very pleased and has booked me for another date next Tuesday night in a variety show which they hold at the 'Palace' every week. I have got special permission from my commanding officer to appear in this show ...

Well darling, now regards to weekend leave, I may manage the week after next, anyway I will let you know in good time. I will probably get away about 12.30 p.m. on Sat. and return here Monday night.

I shall have to find out what the fare will be. I expect it will be quite a bit, anyway, it will be worth it, won't it darling? Will you let me know if Sat. week (April 8th) will be O.K. dear ...

Your loving husband,

Ray. x x x x x x

A postscript is hastily added, however, before this letter is sent.

> *P.S. Have only just found out that all leave on Sat. week (April 8th) is going to be cancelled so I shall try to come next Sat. (April 1st). Please write soon darling.*

The next letter, however, bears disappointing news.

30.3.44.

My own darling wife,

... Now darling about leave. It appears I have been a little too optimistic. I applied today but was told that I cannot be spared, at least not for a week or so. So I'm afraid darling it looks like 'I've had it' for the time being. The trouble seems to be that I happen to be an N.C.O. I suppose that if I hadn't a stripe they would probably have let me go. I tried hard to talk the C.O. into letting me go, but no luck. I am terribly disappointed darling and I know you will be. Still they have promised a weekend so we shan't have to wait too long dear.

Of course, the job we are doing down here is very 'hush hush' and also a special War Office rush effort and must be completed by a certain time ...

Well darling, I'm certainly feeling pretty miserable now. Still there's nothing I can do about it. If I go without permission I should only get into serious trouble and it's not really worth it is it dear? Not for such a short time anyway. We shall have to keep our chins up and it will only probably be about a fortnight until I am saying 'Hello!' darling, so keep smiling dear ...

All my love darling,
Your loving husband,
Ray. x x x x x x

1.4.44.

My own darling wife,

Just a few lines once again. Well darling, it's Sat. night and I'm feeling a little bit 'blue'. I certainly didn't expect to be spending it in Lowestoft. All leave next weekend has been cancelled so I shall probably get away for leave the week after. Anyway I will let you know definitely later on.

We have managed to get a wireless in our billet, so that provides us with a little entertainment in the evenings. We don't get into the town a great deal and generally feel too tired when we do get the chance. In fact we are working all day Sat. and Sunday at the moment.

By the way darling, I forgot to tell you how the show went off last Tuesday. Well, everything went off very well indeed, a very good show including a full band. They certainly rattled out my signature tune ('I Wanna Go Back in the Evening') and the act went over pretty good. Of course all the boys were there again (I think they've been hearing my act for the 500th time) and the applause from them alone made it sound like a riot. Anyway the manager paid me 10/6 for ten minutes which is not to be sneezed at is it darling? Altogether I received 30/6 during last week and bags of free drinks and eats, so I didn't do so badly.

Well darling, I am counting the days until I see you again. It seems years since I said goodbye to you in London dear. What a miserable day that was wasn't it? Still it won't be long my dearest when all goodbyes will be a thing of the past. Roll on that day ...

Your loving husband,
Ray. x x x x x x

The next letter promised another leave date.

5.4.44.

My own darling wife,
... Yes darling I know how disappointed you must have been over last weekend. Still never mind dear, we have still got it to look forward to haven't we?

I have had it on pretty good authority that on April 12th our unit will start another ten days leave. Anyway I'm hoping that it is right ... Well darling, we are still working pretty hard here although we are expecting it to ease up a bit later on ... We can ... obtain one of my weaknesses, can't you guess? Yes, fish and chips! ...

I must say it's a lot better than Brandon here. We are billeted in an old hotel, which is more comfortable than damp, draughty Nissen huts. The food is very good and I've certainly regained that lost appetite. How is the old factory these days darling? You must get fed up with it. I shall be glad when the day comes you can say goodbye to all that. Well my darling, I think that's all for now so I will close once again. With love and regards to Mum and Dad and all my love and kisses to you my darling and God Bless.

Your loving husband,
Ray. x x x x x x

Again, hopes of leave are dashed in the next letter.

9.4.44.

My own darling wife,

... still nothing definite about leave ... I will let you know darling directly I know for sure. It certainly seems a long time waiting doesn't it? It has been miserable here today, raining nearly all day. Roll on the summer! I just can't realise it is another Easter nearly gone ... It seems as though this damn war is never going to finish. I wish something would happen ... By the way darling, I hear the new rates of pay are going to benefit the married men after all ... All boiled down it means that the army pays the wife 10/6 a week ... I'm missing you more each day dear. I spend hours thinking of those few happy days at Milton Hall. It all seems so long ago. Whenever I hear 'Would it Be Wrong to Kiss?' on the wireless (remember it darling?) my thoughts always wander back ...

Your loving husband,
Ray. x x x x x x

12.4.44.

My own darling wife,
... this leave business seems as remote as ever. I don't know what to make of it. As far as I can make out, all leave has been cancelled for us and nobody here at the school is getting any. I shall soon be due for another ten days when it comes and I think it will be started again soon. The only thing we can do dear is to keep smiling and look forward to it. We shall certainly have to make up for all this shan't we darling? I feel pretty miserable these days. I do miss you so dear, especially in the evenings. Roll on the day when we can be together always. I'm glad to hear things are going to be a little easier for you at the factory darling. By the way, I'm looking forward to seeing the new turban darling. They are my weakness and they certainly suit you dear.

The evenings seem long now don't they? Our radio is never switched off (our C.O. is going to get a shock when he sees our electric meter) ...

Your loving husband,
Ray. x x x x x x

P.S. Write again soon dear.
P.P.S. I love you.

A postcard is then written informing Doreen that Ray is in hospital.

Lowestoft.
12.4.44.

Darling, Just a few lines to say I have got a septic leg and am in hospital for a few days. Nothing serious. Writing later.
Love, Ray.

A letter follows two days later.

15.4.44.

My own darling wife,

... It's nothing serious ... I had some sheet metal fall on it a week or so ago and a few days ago it turned septic. It's getting better now though and, as I have said, I shall soon be out. Well darling, I received your letter with the [wedding] *photos in and I think they are quite good don't you? Anyway I had given up hope of any at all, so they came as a very pleasant surprise. By the way, darling, do you mind if I keep them for a day or so? I would like to show them to the boys and I promise to send them back right away. By the way all our mail is being censored once again. No more news about leave yet, but I am still hoping darling. Anyway the days are rolling by and it can't be much longer now ...*

All my love and kisses to you darling. God Bless.

Your loving husband,

Ray. x x x x x x

18.4.44.

My own darling wife,

Just a few lines to let you know that I am back to duty again ... Well still no more news about leave worse luck, in fact we can't even have any relatives down to see us now, not within 15 miles of the coast anyway and so there the matter rests at present ... Well darling, I'm certainly looking forward to this elusive leave. It seems years since Milton Hall doesn't it? There's no need for me to tell you how much I'm missing you, you know that don't you dear? It's a grand day here today, bags of sunshine, just like summer. Where is this war anyway? Probably find out later on! Well darling, no more news this time so will close with all my love and kisses and God Bless,

Your loving husband,

Ray. x x x x x x

P.S. Love and regards to Mum and Dad and remember me to all at Cannock.

21.4.44.

My own darling wife,

... Do you think you will be able to wangle any more time off when I get leave dear? I hope so ...

Your loving husband,

Ray. x x x x x x

28.4.44.

My own darling wife,

... Well dear I think I can manage 47 hours leave next Friday (May 5th) so I'm wondering if it would be best for you to come down to London and meet me or shall I come up to Cannock? I'm afraid darling that if I come all the way, we shall not have a lot of time together, however, please write and let me know as soon as possible won't you dear?

I thought that if you did come and meet me at Liverpool Station, we could fix up bed and breakfast somewhere and have a bit longer to ourselves, anyway, let me know darling ... I'm counting the hours until I see you again ...

Please write soon,

Your loving husband,

Ray. x x x x x x

Ray then sends two telegrams on 2 May 1944. The first states:

LEAVE ALTERED TO WED. MAY 3rd. MEET YOU LIVERPOOL ST. 2.30. TOMORROW. BRING FIVE POUNDS. WIRE TO LET ME KNOW. LOVE, RAY.

All of Doreen's hopes are crushed by another which states:

TERRIBLY SORRY DARLING. LEAVE FOR TOMORROW CANCELLED. IGNORE PREVIOUS TELEGRAM. WRITING. LOVE, RAY.

A letter dated the same day the telegrams were sent explains what had happened.

2.5.44.

My own darling wife,

Well dear there is no need for me to say how bitterly disappointed I am over the complete mix up over my leave and I do hope that my conflicting telegrams did not cause you too much inconvenience. I understood that I could come on Friday for sure, but was told this morning that this had been altered to tomorrow (Wed. May 3rd). I sent a telegram to you dear (which I hope you received O.K.).

I hadn't been back in the office a couple of hours when I heard that all school leave had been cancelled, so I had to rush back again and send another wire to you. I had visions of your coming all the way down to London for nothing and that would have been pretty awful wouldn't it? The whole trouble is darling that we shall probably be back to our units in a couple of days. We are finishing down here a lot sooner than was generally expected, so everything is so unsettled. Anyway everybody has 'had it' as far as leave is concerned ...

Well dear, I'm feeling pretty fed up now over everything. It's the second time this has happened. I certainly seem fated don't I? Still I'm not the only one here and it's really not anyone's fault. I know how disappointed you must have been darling. Still there is a war on and you haven't got to look very far for someone worse off than we are have you dear?

After all, as we have said before, I'm lucky to be back in England.

We shall have to keep smiling and look forward to the 'one day' and I'm sure it's not so very far away now ...

With all my love and kisses, God Bless,

Your loving husband,

Ray. x x x x x x

A postcard reveals that Ray is back with his squadron and it is obvious from the description in the letter that follows that he has not returned to Brandon.

7911536 L/CPL HARRIS R.,
H.Q. Squadron 7th Armoured Division,
A.P.O. Home Forces,
England.

4.5.44.

Darling,
Just a card in haste to let you know my new address (as above) so will you address all your letters to there from now on?

Hoping you have got over the disappointment of my leave darling and that you have received my letter explaining everything. Never mind dear, I still think it won't be long now before I see you. Keep smiling and keep that chin up. Regards to all and all my love and kisses darling,

Ray. x x x x x x

It was in May that the Division was moved to Brentwood and West Ham before the invasion of Normandy.

9.5.44.

My own darling wife,
... It seems a lot colder here than where we have just come from, although quite pleasant on a nice day, real country though. We do get lorries running into the larger towns several times during the week and that makes a bit of a break. Otherwise there is very little in the way of entertainment.

Still, it is paradise compared with being abroad and that's one thing I do appreciate ...

Your loving husband,
Ray. x x x x x x

13.5.44.

My own darling wife,

... Well things are pretty well the same here, in fact, everything is very quiet. The weather is certainly grand, too good to last I think. I can't realize a war is really on, everything is so peaceful. We must be in one of the prettiest spots in England ... By the way darling, 'how's about' having a photo done of yourself, complete with turban? Alright, I know what you are saying, 'What, more photos?' Still you know darling, I can <u>never</u> have too many ... We have our own dance band here now, not bad at all, so we generally have a few swing sessions in the local N.A.A.F.I. It helps to make the evenings go a bit quicker.

These summer nights seem to drag don't they darling? Still, not much longer for us to wait, I hope ...

All my love and kisses to you darling and God Bless.

Your loving husband,

Ray. x x x x x x

18.5.44.

My own darling wife,

Many thanks dear for your letters and parcel received today. The handkerchiefs were very acceptable darling and the cake has gone already and very nice too. I certainly enjoyed it.

Well darling as per usual there's very little to talk about. I've had a very quiet time lately. I did go and see 'Above Suspicion' with Fred MacMurray and Joan Crawford (who, by the way, always reminds me of you).

Not a bad film really, but I had to dash away before the end, to snatch a cup of tea at the local N.A.A.F.I., before they closed. It's no good darling, I just can't break this tea habit ...

Well darling, still no news re leave yet, still I keep hoping. Fancy nearly three months since I last saw you, it doesn't seem possible does it? Don't be surprised to see me turn up unheralded at 74[14] *one of these days ...*

---

14 Doreen was living at 74 Church Street, Chadsmoor, Cannock, Staffordshire

Your loving husband,
Ray. x x x x x x

It is obvious from the next letter that Ray fully expected to be sent home on leave before being posted abroad. He must have realised, however, that time was running out.

25.5.44.

My own darling wife,

... I think you are a little too modest about your cooking darling. All the boys agreed it was a very good effort.

Well darling, I don't know what is happening about leave. I'm getting a little fed up being away from my wife so long. After all it's not natural is it dear? I am missing you so much my dear and my only interest in life now is to get home with you once again my darling and tell you how much you mean to me. Still, as you say dear, we have all our happy days to look forward to. Days when I will be able to come home at night and find you waiting for me. Won't it be wonderful darling? Together for always! It's only this thought that keeps me going and I'm praying it won't be long now before we both realize these dreams.

I note what you say about the hair cream darling and I would be pleased if you can get it for me. I've been pretty busy today doing my own washing. Can you beat it? Anyway I have struggled manfully over one shirt, two pairs of socks and a couple of towels and used a couple of bars of soap doing them. What a life! ...

Goodnight my darling and God Bless,
Your loving husband,
Ray. x x x x x x

By 28 May 1944, the Division was fully prepared for the next stage of the war and the next letter bearing the same date suggests that Ray had been briefed that the voyage to France was imminent.

28.5.44.

My own darling wife,

... Well darling, chances of leave seem rather remote at the moment. Nobody is getting any.

I think the 8th Army chaps you have seen must be stationed round that way. Still we must be patient I suppose and keep smiling. I think we have waited so many years that a few more months should go quickly shouldn't they darling?

I do hope that you are not too miserable dear, after all the disappointments over leave. I must confess I get very depressed at times but we are married and that's a step forward from a year ago isn't it? All I know darling, is that we will more than make up for all this very soon now. Until then, you know I am always thinking of you darling and looking towards the day when letters between us will be just a thing of the past. So Goodnight dearest and God Bless.

All my love and kisses to you darling,

Your loving husband,

Ray. x x x x x x

The next letter is undated but probably is the last written before Ray set sail for France.

My own darling wife,

It's Sunday evening and I'm feeling a little lonely. I feel that I simply must write to you my dearest. These few lines may appear a little different from my usual run of letters darling, perhaps a bit more sentimental. News is so scarce that I hardly know what to write about as a rule, so here's a letter darling telling you how much I love you and miss you.

There's still no news of leave yet but I am praying it won't be long before I am holding you in my arms once again dear. I do miss you so my darling, but I feel very contented as I know we have one another for always and have countless happy days to look forward to. I know we are going to be happy together my dearest and you know I love you with all my heart and always will.

I shall always remember too those very happy days we spent together on our honeymoon ... Everything has happened so suddenly hasn't it? Thousands of miles away from one another one day and married the next. Still I know that neither of us is going to regret that grand day of Feb. 26th because we love one another and that's all that really matters.

Well darling, I shall have to say Goodnight dearest and God Bless. With all my love and kisses,

Your loving husband,

Ray. x x x x x x

During the months before the invasion the RAF had bombed railways and bridges on the Continent. To facilitate the landings, huge 'Mulberries' (floating harbours) were sailed across from Britain. 'Pluto', a pipe line laid under the sea, provided petrol.

7911536. L/CPL. HARRIS. R.
H.Q Squadron,
7TH ARMOURED DIVISION,
A.P.O. ENGLAND.

My own darling wife,
Its Sunday evening, + feeling a little lonely I feel that I simply must write to you my dearest.
These few lines may appear a little differant from my usual run of letters darling, perhaps a bit more sentimental.
News is so scarce, that I hardly know what to write about as a rule, so heres a letter darling telling you how much I love you + missing you.
Theres still no news of leave yet

The last letter, probably written before Ray set sail for Normandy.

Sketch map of Normandy

Chapter 8

D-Day and the French Campaign

On 4 June 1944, the Allied army embarked for France from various points around Britain. Ray probably left from Dovercourt on 5 June. The huge convoy of ships sailed into a strong wind. By 6 June, the Normandy coast was sighted. The plan was to land 170,000 men supported by 3,000 guns, 1,500 tanks and 15,000 various transport. These would attack the German Panzer forces under Rommel who held the French coastline from Antwerp to the River Orne and from there to the River Loire. The RAF bombed the coast near Normandy beach on the evening of D-Day (6 June). Ray drove his tank off the tank landing craft straight into seawater and then on to Sword Beach on the same day. The landing caught the Germans off guard and the attack against the British grew in intensity the following night. Throughout, the 7th Arm'd Div. was at the forefront of battle.

The first goal was to procure a bridgehead, containing Caen and Bayeux, and land westwards. The countryside, a few yards inland from the beach, was clearing and marshland. Beyond this, the main area for the conflict was the Bocage. This consisted of square miles of fields, farms and villages. Thirty miles south of Bayeux, it was heavily wooded with dense hedges, high trees and crops and narrow roads, an extremely trying landscape in which to manoeuvre a tank.

From 9 June onwards, there was unceasing, fierce enemy opposition. Despite this, many positions were successfully captured. On 10 June the Division was ordered to advance on Tilly where there was more bitter fighting.

On 12 June 1944, Ray sent an official Field Service postcard bearing two statements:

I AM QUITE WELL, LETTER FOLLOWS AT FIRST OPPORTUNITY.
R.A.J. HARRIS.

A letter was written the same day.

12.6.44.

My own darling wife,
Well dear, I suppose you have guessed why I have been unable to write this last week or so. Now darling, I do hope you haven't been worrying too much as I am quite well. Everything has gone very well and the only thing I am allowed to tell you is that we are somewhere in France. Anyway, there is nothing at all to worry about dear and I feel sure it won't be long now before we are together for good. So keep smiling darling! I shall be looking forward to the photo dear. Did it turn out alright? Please forgive this rather short letter but am anxious you get it as soon as possible. Will write again soon. Love and regards to Mum and Dad and all my love and kisses to you my darling and God Bless.

Your loving husband,
Ray. x x x x x x

(Army Form A. 2042.)
(R.A.F. Form No. 1929)

FIELD SERVICE

POST CARD

The address only to be written on this side. If anything else is added the post card will be destroyed.

[Crown Copyright Reserved.]

PASSED BY CENSOR No. 2007

Mrs. D. Harris,
14 Church St,
Chadsmoor,
CANNOCK,
Staffs
England

NOTHING is to be written on this side except the date and signature of the sender. Sentences not required may be erased. If anything else is added the post card will be destroyed.

[Postage must be prepaid on any letter or post card addressed to the sender of this card.]

I am quite well.

~~I have been admitted into hospital~~

~~sick~~ / ~~wounded~~ ~~and am going on well.~~ / ~~and hope to be discharged soon.~~

~~I am being sent down to the base.~~

~~I have received your~~ ~~letter dated~~ / ~~telegram~~ ,, / ~~parcel~~ ,,

Letter follows at first opportunity.

~~I have received no letter from you~~

~~lately~~ / ~~for a long time.~~

Signature only: Ray Harris.

Date 12/6/44.

Forms/A2042/7. 51-4997.

The Field Service postcard informing Doreen that Ray had survived D-Day.

After the first major battle, called the Battle of Villers-Bocage (when the Allies successfully fought off a fierce German assault), the Allies found themselves in advantageous positions in the villages west of Villers-Bocage. This took place between 13 and 15 June. The Division fought with great courage and suffered many casualties.

Ray wrote a short letter on 15 June repeating much of what he had written in the previous one and reassuring Doreen:

'I am not so far away, so we shall both have to keep smiling ... don't worry as I am perfectly O.K.'

Unbeknown to Doreen there had been many losses and 27 tanks destroyed.

On 17 June, large numbers of German forces were crushed in bitter fighting at Briquessard. The Division then withdrew to an area behind the Briquessard ridge for the rest of the month.

It was a very demanding period, spent in slit trenches suffering much shelling and mortar attack. There had to be constant vigilance resulting in little sleep. There continued to be many casualties.

17.6.44.

My own darling wife,

... I am returning a few of the photos darling, as I find it rather difficult keeping them clean and I don't want to get them spoilt as they will be with all the rain we have been having lately. I am keeping the two latest of yourself dear as I can keep them in my wallet ...

Yes, darling, I was very pleased to hear from Vera and to know that Brighton has been more or less without the 'doodle bugs' ...

I am certainly looking forward to the new hairstyle dear. Is it anything like the last one? I thought it suited you very well.

Anyway write and try and describe this latest one will you darling?

Well! We are on our sixth week in France now. The days certainly go don't they? I honestly think that it will soon be all over in Europe anyway.

As you say darling, it will be great getting back to Brighton again and not having to worry about leave passes or trains. It certainly will be a little strange for me after so long in the army. Anyway I know it won't take us long to settle down together to start a very happy married life.

By the way darling, if you can't get any books, I would rather like the 'Stage' or the 'Performer' sent out each week. You could let Dad read them first and then send them on to me. They only cost about 3d or 4d although I expect you would have to order them ... Still counting the days until I am with you for always.

Your loving husband,

Ray. x x x x x x

P.S. Excuse pencil and this horrible paper but everything is pretty scarce in the way of writing material until N.A.A.F.I. arrives darling.

18.6.44.

My own darling wife,

Many thanks for your letters, hair cream, papers and most of all darling, your photo which I think is <u>very good indeed</u> and very charming. I <u>am</u> pleased with it.

The new turban looks very chic darling and I notice the R.A.C. badge is still very much to the fore. I like to see you wearing it dear. Well darling, I do hope you are not going to worry about me out here. Everything is O.K. I thought that perhaps you may have guessed that I should have to go, but of course I couldn't write and tell you. I expect you were all pretty excited about 'D' Day weren't you? It was quite an event. It certainly had its tragedies and, funnily enough, its humorous moments. Anyway

I can't tell you much darling but will leave it until the censor is a little kinder to us.

You know dearest I am always thinking of you and loving you. I know we can both keep our chins up and keep smiling because we know that we have everything in life before us and thousands of happy days. I know that all these months of waiting will make us both appreciate everything that a happy marriage has to offer and, as you know darling, it is certainly a lot. I don't think we shall have so long to wait now my dearest and when the one day comes we shall be able to look back and say that it was all certainly worth waiting for.

It won't take us long to settle down and I have always my job at Lawsons waiting for me if I want it, so we shan't have a lot to worry about in that direction shall we?

It's just like old times again out here as you may guess. Reminds me of that very old song 'Back to Those Happy (?!) Days.'

Anyway darling, please write and say you are not going to worry about anything. Before we know where we are, we shall be back together again for always.

I will write as often as I possibly can dear but, once again, don't worry if you don't hear regularly sometimes. You will know that we are moving so much that the mail will probably be a bit late ...

Your loving husband,
Ray. x x x x x x

P.S. The hair tonic was just the stuff I wanted, thanks a lot darling.

7911536 Cpl. HARRIS. R.
H.Q SQUADRON 7th ARMOURED DIVISION.
A.P.O ENGLAND.
18.6.44.

My own darling wife,

Many thanks for your letters, haversack papers + most of all darling, your photo which I think is very good indeed + very charming. I am pleased with it. The new turban looks very chic darling, + I notice the R.A.C badge is still very much to the fore, I like to see you wearing it dear. Well darling, I do hope you are not going to worry about me out here, everything is O.K. I thought that perhaps you may have guessed that I should have to go, but of course I couldn't write + tell you.

I expect you were all pretty excited about D day weren't you? It was quite an event. It certainly had its tradgedies + funnily enough its humourous moments, anyway, I can't tell you much darling, but will leave it

②

until the censor is a little kinder to us. You know dearest, I am always thinking of you + loving you, I know we can both keep our chins up, + keep smiling, because we know that we have everything in life before us, + thousands of happy days. I know that all these months of waiting will make us both appreciate everything that a happy marriage has to offer, + as you know darling, it is certainly a lot.

I don't think we shall have so long to wait now, my dearest, + when the one day comes we shall be able to look back + say that it was all certainly worth waiting for.

It won't take us long to settle down, + I have always my job at Lawsons waiting for me if I want it, so we shan't have a lot to worry about in that direction shall we?

It's just like old times again out here now

3

as you may guess reminds me of that very old song "Back to those happy? days", anyway darling please write + say you are not going to worry about anything, and before we know where we are we shall be back together again for always.

I will write as often as I possibly can dear, but once again don't worry if you don't hear regularly sometimes, you will know that we are moving so much that the mail will probably be a bit late.

Must close now with love + regards to mum + dad, + all my love + kisses to you my darling + God Bless,

Your loving husband

Ray

xxxxxxxxxxxxxxxxxxxxxx
xxxxxxxxxxxxxxxxxxxxxx
xxxxxxxxxxxxxxxxxxxxxxxx

P.S. The hair tonic was just the stuff I wanted thanks a lot darling.

One of Ray's letters written to Doreen after D-Day, dated 18.06.1944

20.6.44.

My own darling wife,

... Your letter today has cheered me up a lot darling. As you say it is really a great deal to know we are really married and my darling 'You Will Really Be Wonderful to Come Home to' or how does the popular song go?

I am counting the days until you are really in my arms again my sweet and feeling your lips so close to my face. We shall laugh and say maybe it hasn't been so long to wait, after all. We are both going to be so happy darling and are going to have some wonderful times when this nightmare is over. So, as you say, we can keep our chins up and smile over the last few months ...

Your loving husband,

Ray. x x x x x x

P.S. Am enclosing a white carnation I picked from a little farm somewhere in Normandy. Just a souvenir. I thought you may like it darling.

26.6.44.

My own darling wife,

... I do hope we shall both always be very much in love and always have time to be sentimental and I hope we shall never change ...

The weather has been really hot lately and you would be surprised how sunburnt we have become in such a short time. By the way darling thanks for the papers also. If you want to read a glowing account of the Division try and get the Daily Sketch dated 22/6/44 ...

Goodnight my dearest and God Bless,

Your loving husband,

Ray. x x x x x x

By the end of June the Division had formed a liaison with the Americans who shared their equipment. By the end of the month it handed over completely to the Americans who took Cherbourg on 26 June. During three weeks in Normandy, the Division had lost 1,149 men.

By July, the Allies had formed a strong beach-head to launch more operations. One million Allied troops had landed on the beach area which was by now dense with men, vehicles and equipment. The Germans by this time were considerably weakened. By 10 July Caen had been taken, 17 July the ground between Tilly and Caen and 18 July Saint-Lô (by the Americans).

Letters in this early period of July (dated 2.7.44, 6.7.44, 8.7.44 and 11.7.44) continue to reassure Doreen and reveal that Ray is constantly on the move.

8.7.44.

We have been so busy moving at a moment's notice, sometimes in the middle of the night and early morning.

Despite this, he is able to scrounge a few bars of chocolate for Vera and Eddie's son, Peter.

Two more letters are written before the next major battle. These are dated 13 and 16 July 1944.

13.7.44.

My own darling wife,

... I heard from Vera today, at last. I was relieved in a way, what with these flying bombs around and Brighton being more or less in the danger area ...

Well my darling, your letters are coming through to me regularly now and they certainly cheer me up and help me to keep smiling along ...

I think one day we will take a trip to Bramber. Remember darling? How long ago that is isn't it? I wonder if the old swings are still there. I think perhaps Fate knew that we really cared for one another then, even if it was so long ago, don't you darling?

I can hardly realize it is so long as February since I kissed you 'Goodbye' and yet it seems years. I do long for you so much darling ...

Your ever loving husband,
Ray. x x x x x x

P.S. I believe you can send cigarettes out here at a very cheap rate, so if you could manage a few darling, they would be very acceptable as smokes are very scarce. I always seem to smoke more during campaigns. Must keep the morale up I suppose. x R.

Over the next spell of fierce fighting during 'Operation Goodwood' (18 to 20 July) there are no letters. The operation took place southeast of Caen in countryside very different from the Bocage. The area was mainly made up of farmland enclosed by woodland and apple trees ascending to the Bourguébus ridge. The enemy was still strong along this ridge and also between the Rivers Orne and Dives.

The purpose of this operation was (1) to involve the 7th Arm'd Div. (supporting the 11th Division and Guards) in engaging the enemy to assist the American breakout at the Cherbourg Peninsula, (2) to facilitate the advance to the Seine and (3) to damage the enemy as much as possible.

Ray's division had to be moved over the River Orne. This proved very difficult as there were many mines and insufficient bridges. On 18 July they moved over amidst dust and shell fire. 19 July saw intense enemy shelling of the Orne bridges and many tanks caught fire. Despite strong opposition, over 2,000 German prisoners were taken and 60 enemy tanks disabled. On 20 July there was a very violent cloudburst. Trenches were flooded and tanks unable to move through the mud. The assault was therefore halted and the Division confined to limited cover. Here it was an easy target for the enemy. The Germans were able to observe all its movements.

Between 20 and 24 July the Division suffered relentless shelling and there were many casualties and much damage to vehicles. Tank crews often had to take shelter in the tanks during the day. The Germans also sent bombers over but the RAF supported the Allies.

There is one letter from this period, dated 22 July 1944, thanking Doreen for letters and books. Ray writes:

> *I will pass them round among the lads, as reading material is always appreciated.*

The next three, dated 25, 26 and 28 July 1944, reveal nothing of the danger and hardships of the next stage of the Campaign. Ray mentions in the first that he has heard from Lawsons, his former place of employment.

> *I had a reply from Lawsons, quite a nice letter expressing the hope that the war will soon be over and about my going back to them.*

'Operation Spring' (25 to 29 July) saw the Division face more shelling and mortar attack in a defensive position supporting the Canadians as they made a bid to gain ground east of Orne and the north road from Caen to Falaise. On 28 July the Division handed over to the Canadians. Again, many vehicles had been damaged and 400 men killed since the middle of the month.

By now the Americans had broken out of the Cherbourg Peninsula (25 July), greatly helped by the 7th Arm'd Div. occupying the enemy whilst this was achieved. On 27 July the Germans started to retreat on the American front.

The next two letters were written during 'Operation Bluecoat' (30 July and 10 August). The Division wasn't needed at the start but on 30 July moved northeast of Caumont.

31.7.44.

My own darling wife,

... I suppose you are just starting your holiday now darling. I hope you are getting as nice weather as we are now having in France. These last two days we have had real sunshine and it's really hot. I only hope it continues so that we can get this campaign over and get back home, as all the rain we have had lately has certainly slowed things up. Yes the news is certainly very promising and I don't think it will be long now before we are together again dearest ...

Well darling our canteen has been up today and we are now the proud possessors of one bottle of beer per man, one razor blade and some cigs. So tonight we are making beasts of ourselves on the one bottle!

We have an inter squadron football match tonight. I shan't be playing myself (after nearly breaking my leg scoring a goal in the last match) but will probably turn out and give the lads vocal support ...

It seems years since we were together darling. I am always thinking of those few happy days we had together at Brighton.

All my love and kisses to you my darling and God Bless,

Your loving husband,

Ray. x x x x x x

The next letter, dated 3 August 1944, was written during further action. It refers to Doreen's holiday in Coventry and the mail being held up for five days. On 1 August the Division had joined Montgomery's 'Operation Bluecoat'. This was planned to help the American advance in a thick part of the Bocage. For six weeks there had been no Allied attack there and the Germans had succeeded in building up defences. The aim of the British army was to capture Mont Pinçon (south of Aunay-sur-Odon).

Further gains for the Allies distracted the enemy from the Americans and prevented more troops being built against them. On 8 August Mont Pinçon was taken.

The last days in the Bocage were spent between 8 and 10 August. The Germans had tried to cut off the Americans' movement into the middle of France on 7 August at Mortain. The Germans managed to capture it but the Allied air force destroyed most of the enemy left in Normandy.

The 7th Arm'd Div. advanced on Condé and small gains were made but the terrain made it difficult for the tanks to move. By 9 August they were exhausted and depleted, having been in active service since 18 July.

The Division, therefore, was on 10 August moved back a few miles to rest camps. During this short break Ray writes two letters.

11.8.44.

My own darling wife,

... we are having a real heat wave at the moment. I think of nothing darling but you and the day it all ends ... By the way darling I think I have a few pounds in credit, so I may send some home. This is done through the army. A form is sent to you and you simply cash it at the post office so no actual money is sent through the post and therefore can't be lost ...

Your ever loving husband,

Ray. x x x x x x

The second letter mentions entertainment provided for the Division.

13.8.44.

My own darling wife,

... I have sent £10 home to you ... Well darling the news is great just now and the general opinion is another two months ...

We had our first E.N.S.A. show here yesterday. I didn't go myself but some of the lads went and said it wasn't too bad.

I don't think anybody takes much interest in shows these

days. There's only one finale they want to see and that's the curtain falling on the show out here and I feel the same way too … Roll on the end.

Your ever loving husband,
Ray. x x x x x x

Chapter 9

On to the Seine

The Division's rest was short-lived and on 15 August it was called from the camps to lead the advance (with the Canadian Army) to the Seine 65 miles away. The advance was from the area east of the Caen–Falaise road: an old dusty fly- and mosquito-ridden battlefield. There were many rivers to cross as they followed the retreating enemy. Progress was slow as not only did they meet with resistance, but there were many mines and destroyed bridges in their path.

By 19 August they reached Livarot and were greeted by ecstatic French crowds. There was a fierce battle at Lisieux from 22 to 23 August. By 24 August they passed through to the sounds of cheering civilians and church bells ringing.

From 24 to 25 August there was more fighting as the Division cleared the land up to the Seine. On the same day Ray writes:

24.8.44.

My own darling wife,

At last I have a few more moments to write again. Things have certainly been up and doing out here recently and I can't remember ever moving so often in such a short time. We are hardly in a place a few moments before we get orders to repack and move again. All the lettermail seems to have been held up again darling but I have received the cigs ... Well darling the news is still good isn't it? With Paris falling and a general advance all round ...

The weather has changed a bit today, quite a lot of rain. We don't mind dull and cloudy nights as they don't encourage 'Jerry' bombers over. We are on fresh rations now so we do very well for food and bags of tea, which suits me, as you may guess darling.

Our efforts at cooking even go as far as making suet puddings and one of our chaps is quite an expert, a regular Mr. Beeton in fact ...

Yes dear, I certainly think it calls for a holiday after this lot and if I never see a plane, gun or tank, ever again it will still be too soon. I'm fed up with the sight of them.

Still we must keep smiling along mustn't we darling? ...

All my love and kisses darling and God Bless.

Your ever loving husband,

Ray. x x x x x x

On 25 August the Seine was crossed and the Division stopped for some rest and maintenance. The Allies had won the Battle of Normandy. Half a million Germans had been lost and 10,000 prisoners had been taken. Ray had travelled 220 miles.

28.8.44.

My own darling wife,

... Well dear the news is still good isn't it? I spend most of the time wondering how long it will be now before I am back with you dearest for always. I can't understand how 'Jerry' has lasted as long as he has done. He definitely has taken a terrible bashing out here. Still one of these days I know will be Victory day. What a grand day it will be too, eh darling? ... Yes darling it's over six months now since we were married and living away from you all this time makes it seem like six years ... I can't get anything out here. I'm hoping to get a few presents later on when we get to the bigger towns. Up to now all we have seen is rubble and burning ruins. I'm afraid France is paying heavily for her release.

Still the people keep smiling and carrying on. Thank God that England was never invaded, if all this out here counts for anything ...

Your ever loving husband,
Ray. x x x x x x

On 29 August the Division moved to a château near Le Neuberg.

29.8.44.

My own darling wife,
Many thanks for all your letters received O.K. dear ... We have been on the go all the time this week or so and haven't had five minutes to call our own. Don't worry darling if you don't hear from me so regularly during the next week or so ...

Well darling, things are still going very well now aren't they? The end's not far off ...

The weather is still grand here, bags of sun and everybody is in a good mood, except 'Jerry' of course ...

My love and kisses to you my darling and God Bless.

Your ever loving husband,
Ray. x x x x x x

P.S. Excuse terrible writing but we are on the move again.

Chapter 10

ADVANCE TO GHENT

On 30 August orders were given to begin the advance to Ghent. Each tank had to carry 40 gallons of extra fuel. The journey began on 31 August at three o'clock in the morning. All along the route, the liberators were cheered wildly. On 1 September, through the night, more opposition was met as the 7th Arm'd Div. tanks crossed the Somme.

2 September saw continued enemy action in the Pas de Calais. Despite the supply of petrol and maps running low, the Allies crossed the River Authie. On 3 September, Lille was liberated from the Germans.

3.9.44.

My own darling wife,

... Well dear, we are still moving fast all day and night sometimes.

I can't tell you anything about recent events, of course, but I can tell you the latest one the old Div. is in will be military history when it is published in the papers.

What a difference in the map of France now eh darling? Things are certainly going splendidly and I'm sure 'Jerry' will never stand the pace. I am so longing for the 'Cease Fire' to sound. It is bitterly cold today and we can all feel Winter coming on, still I hope to be home before the real thing arrives ... You know, my dearest, I am always thinking of you and loving you and praying for the one day my darling when we shall be together for always...

Your ever loving husband,
Ray. x x x x x x

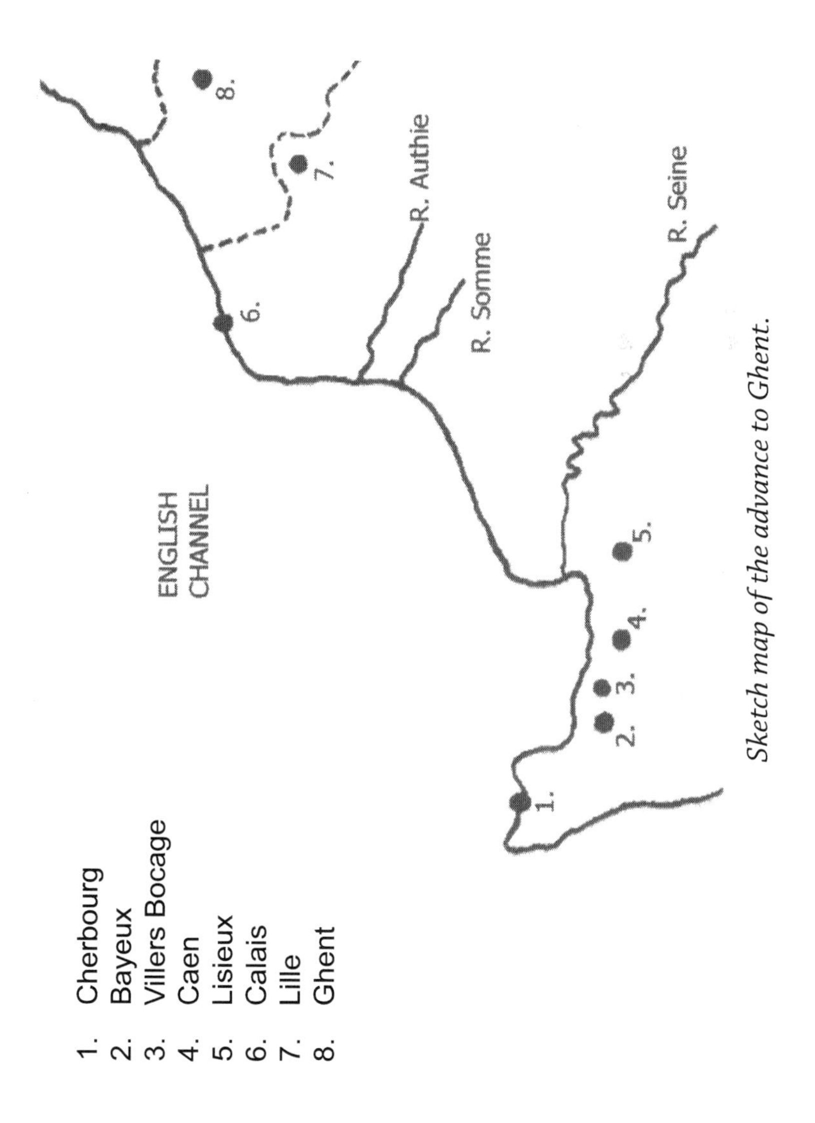

Sketch map of the advance to Ghent.

On 4 September the Division moved west of Lille. As they crossed the frontier into Belgium, cheering crowds showered the Allies with flowers, wine, apples and pears in great jubilation.

The advance continued at dawn on 5 September and there were sporadic outbursts of fighting. The headquarters was moved to a château at Sotteghem, southeast Ghent.

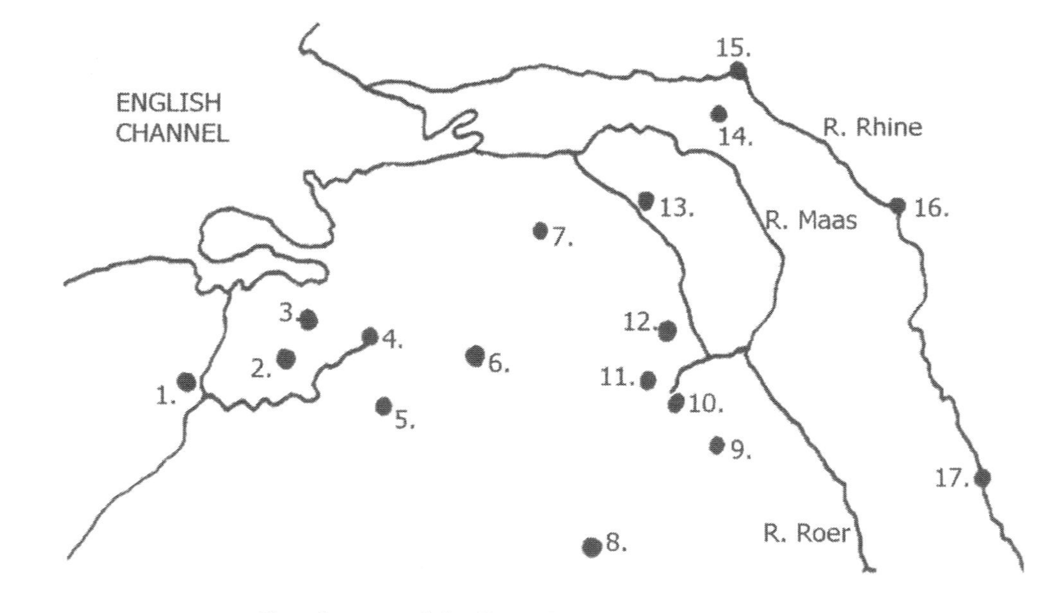

Sketch map of the Low Countries

1. Ghent
2. Lokeren
3. St Nicholas
4. Antwerp
5. Malines
6. Herenthals
7. Tilburg
8. Liège
9. Sittard
10. Maesyck
11. Bree
12. Weert
13. Veghel
14. Reichswald
15. Arnhem
16. Wesel
17. Cologne

Chapter 11

The Low Countries

For the next few days following 6 September, the areas that had been taken around Ghent were made secure though some shelling continued.

8.9.44.

My own darling wife,

Many thanks, dear for the parcel containing 'Brylcreem' etc. ... I think that I shall have to hide the 'Brylcreem' some place otherwise the crowd I'm with will probably be lining up for 'buckshee' dips in. Well darling the news is still good and we have certainly travelled some distance since I last wrote a day or two ago.

I hope to goodness we don't have to spend another winter of War as I believe they have some real Winters here and bags of rain, snow and frost. I am always thinking of you darling and a nice warm bed ...

You know that I'm always loving you my dearest one and praying for the day when I see you again. So keep smiling darling. It won't be long now ...

Your ever loving husband,

Ray. x x x x x x

On 9 September there were rumours of Hitler's abdication. By this time 11 German divisions had massed between Deynze and Audenarde for a desperate attack against the

Allies. In preparation for this, many bridges over the Lys were destroyed. The 7th Arm'd Div. spread out east of Ghent and then cleared Lokeren and Saint-Nicolas. There was still much fighting west of Antwerp and German prisoners were still being taken. More enemy fire occurred as the dock and factory areas north of Ghent were cleared but on 11 September the Poles took over the area. On 13 September the Division moved to Malines and took over the line on the canal between Herentals and Antwerp before the Canadians relieved them.

From this time onwards, up until November, the Division experienced a lack of infantry. Sometimes the tank crews had to be used on foot patrols. It is very possible that Ray was involved in this arrangement. The surrounding countryside was gloomy, flat marshland characterised by canals, dykes and ditches. The Dutch, however, like the French, were warm and friendly. There was still considerable resistance as the canals were crossed.

Ray's letters are less frequent during this period but the following was written as the Battle of Arnhem was starting. This continued until 24 September. Enemy resistance was greater than expected.

14.9.44.

My own darling wife,

... Well darling, things are still going grand out here and the silver lining is definitely in sight ...

We have really been hard at it lately and I am feeling a bit tired now but, as all the boys say, we will carry on day and night until the end ...

We have entered into new territory these days (I can't tell you where) and the people are certainly giving us a grand reception. They all appear to have had a pretty bad time during the German Occupation. Some of them speak a little English but the majority don't so we spend most of our time trying to understand what the conversation is all about ... I am on guard once again tonight so am having plenty of time during the night to think of the happy days ahead of us both ...

Fondest love and kisses to you my dearest darling and God Bless.

Your ever loving husband,
Ray. x x x x x x

19.9.44.

My own darling wife,

... Well darling, since I wrote last, we have been told that we can tell you where we are now. As you have probably guessed dear, we are somewhere in Belgium ... Everyone seems very pleased to see us. You can guess how far we have travelled this last week or so. Some distance eh darling? ...

It will be grand darling when you can say 'goodbye' to that factory dear and pack the old grips for Brighton. I honestly think that the war is now a matter of weeks, so you can soon begin packing darling! ...

I am always loving you and thinking of you every hour ...

Your ever loving husband,
Ray. x x x x x x

The next time Ray wrote at length was after the tanks had reached Veghel on 27 September. The Division forced the enemy back and then crossed the canal. An area of 14 miles (from Veghel to the Maas) was held for a month, until the last week in October. There were many more casualties during this time. The weather was cold and damp and the Allies came under much shelling and mortar attack.

29.9.44.

My own darling wife,

... By the way darling I had a letter from Donald Peers[15] *of all people. I wrote to him ages ago and he sent me an autographed*

15 A popular singer of the time

photo and a very pleasant letter ... Yes I saw the demob. chart and as you say I should be among Group 24. The new rate of pay is just the job isn't it?

I shall be looking forward to the eight weeks leave with pay etc., they are promising us, especially as I get an extra day for every month served abroad.

I notice you mentioned the local girls give us a good welcome. Well, I suppose they do in a way, but they all appear to our lads to be very plain and unattractive.

I can assure you darling, that English girls have nothing to worry about as regards to competition. There is only one girl I am interested in at the moment and she is in Cannock. I'm hoping it won't be long now before I am holding her in my arms and telling her how much I love her ...

Life still is about the same out here. We still keep moving, sometimes at night. It's getting a little monotonous. Still we all keep smiling and say to ourselves it can't last much longer.

Well darling, I shall have to close once again. With love and regards to Mum and Dad and all my love and kisses to you my darling and God Bless.

Your ever loving husband,
Ray. x x x x x x

The letter from Donald Peers was written from Blackpool Pier.

18.9.44.

Dear L/Cpl Harris,
Of all the letters I've ever received, especially from service men, yours was by far the most amazing! Every detail in it was correct and I count myself very lucky to have such a keen follower. Here then are some photos for you, 7 in all, and I hope it won't be long until the day comes when you can, as you say, sit back and enjoy a show once again.

I too had a share of service life, in fact it was just a matter of 25 days short of 4 years. I was discharged on 'D' day and said day is now known in my household as 'Donald's Day'. How are you off for cigs. or soap or any other little things which can be quickly sent over? Let me know and I'll arrange for a supply to follow you around. Let me hear from you now and then. Your letter was most welcome.

Kind regards,

Donald Peers.

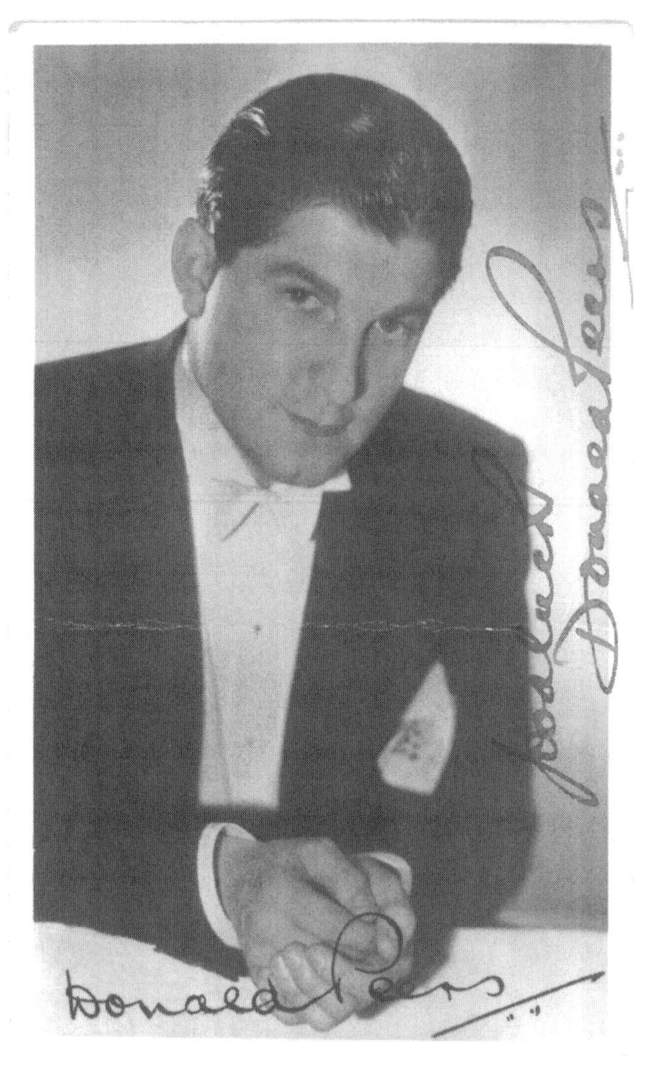

Donald Peers.

Donald Peers
Sole Direction and Business Manager,
GERARD HEATH,
~~Coventry House, 5 & 6, Coventry Street,~~
~~London, W.1.~~

South Pier. Blackpool. SS.
18/9/44.

Dear L/Cpl. Harris.

Of all the letters I've ever received, — especially from service men — yours was by far the most amazing! Every detail in it was correct, and I count myself very lucky to have such a keen follower. Here then are some photos for you. 7 in all, and I hope it won't be long until the day comes when you can, as you say, sit back & enjoy a show once again.

I, too had a share of service life, in fact it was just a matter of 25 days short of 4 years. I was discharged on 'D' day & said day is now known in my household as "Donald's Day". How are you off for eggs. or soap. or any other little thing which can be quickly sent over. — Let me know & I'll arrange for a supply to follow you around.

Let me hear from you now & then, — your letter was most welcome.

Kind regards
Donald Peers

Send letters c/o
Ger. Heath.
new address.
how did you get it ??

Donald Peers's letter to Ray (18.09.1944).

1.10.44.

My own darling wife,
... I've never known the time to drag so much not even in the desert. I suppose it is because we are all so optimistic, don't you darling? A case of a 'watched pot never boils' ...

6.10.44.

... Well dear, at the moment we are having a few days rest and on Sunday we are giving a concert once again, the first one since we came home from Italy. I have promised to do an act and am at the moment doing a spot of rehearsal. We have been lucky enough to find a nice little hall complete with stage lighting and seating ...

12.10.44.

... Well darling the show ... went over really big. We gave three performances starting on Sunday night and of course all the 'big noises' of the Division were present including the General, who, by the way, was so pleased with the show that he saw it through twice and personally congratulated me on my effort.

I rounded up a few of the ex-'Strollers' and produced the whole show in just over two days. As we gave a two hours non-stop show, you can guess I had a very busy time ...

I wonder how much longer it will be now before the end? ... Still, in spite of stiff opposition, bad weather and minor set backs, I still think it will be over by November. Keep praying for it darling ...

16.10.44.

... Well we have given one show since I wrote last and that was given to one of our units. We actually gave the performance within two miles of the Germans. Still everything went off great, in spite of us being a bit close. I fully expected to see a few 'Jerries' come in during the show and sit down in the audience. I am writing this in bed and the light isn't any too good, so please

excuse the bad writing dear.

We have fixed a canteen up here and can get plenty of Dutch beer which isn't much good as it is really ersatz stuff made from beet ...

Your ever loving husband,
Ray. x x x x x x

By the time the next batch of letters were written the Division had moved on. The Allies were unable to use Antwerp port as the north and south banks of the Scheldt Estuary were under German control. There was, therefore, an all-out effort to take the areas approaching Antwerp from the enemy. However, the next letter reveals that action was yet to begin.

24.10.44.

My own darling wife,
... Well things are very quiet here just now and the other night I was able to take the boys along and give an American Hospital a couple of hours show and did those Yanks enjoy it!

They literally fetched the roof off and yelled for more. They were definitely the best audience I have played to in years. It was probably the first show they had had in months, as the hospital is off the beaten track and of course misses any entertainment in the way of mobile cinemas or E.N.S.A. shows. Anyway, they certainly lapped it up. The boys all voted it was really a pleasure playing to them ...

The Winter seems to be coming in now doesn't it? Let's hope that we get no snow. Just fancy only about nine weeks to Xmas. I wonder whether I shall make it? ... I am missing you terribly dearest and praying for the day when I can tell you how much I love you.

Your ever loving husband,
Ray. x x x x x x
P.S. Glad to hear your cold is better. Take care of yourself darling, R. x

When Ray writes next, the Division is up to the Maas. In the last week of October 110 men and 22 tanks had been lost but 900 German prisoners taken.

31.10.44.

My own darling wife,

... Things seem to be going O.K., if a trifle slow. I do wish something would happen inside Germany, so they would pack it in ... I'm glad that I have got quite a bit of overseas service now, as I know there is going to be a very big call up for Burma after this lot is over and I certainly wouldn't like to land up there ... Somehow, I still think that the end will come suddenly and we shall probably be dazed when it does come, I know I shall! ... Keep that chin up ...

Your ever loving husband,
Ray. x x x x x x

Between 1 and 10 November there was no fighting with the enemy. There was a period of rest and training and the tanks were given a service. The divisional headquarters were based at Tilburg where the people were well off and very hospitable. The weather was bitterly cold and the Division was issued with weatherproof clothing called 'zoot suits'. These had a number of ingenious zips which enabled them to be used as sleeping bags.

3.11.44.

My own darling wife,

... Well darling, I think it would be a very good idea if you can find a job at Brighton ... Do you think that they would let you leave the factory? It would be great to think that you were at Brighton again and to know that I could come straight to you ...

I have the unenviable job of orderly corporal at the moment,

chasing everybody for guards and fatigues, still I get by O.K. ...
Love and kisses to you my darling and God Bless.
Your ever loving husband,
Ray. x x x x x x x

On 10 November the Division took over the line along the Maas and Wessem Canal.

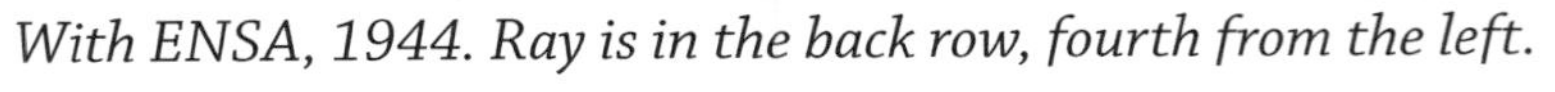

With ENSA, 1944. Ray is in the back row, fourth from the left.

Chapter 12

Ray's Tour with ENSA

The next batch of letters finds Ray involved once more with a show. It would be the first time that he had the opportunity to appear with professional artistes in ENSA.

18.11.44.

My own darling wife,

Many thanks for gloves, soap and blades which I received yesterday. I am so pleased with the gloves darling. They are very nice indeed and I can certainly use them especially as the days are getting very cold now. Well dear things are very quiet with us again and these dull November days seem to drag a bit. However, next week Major Cobbald (my commanding officer) has arranged for me to go out on a week's tour with an E.N.S.A. show who apparently are very short of artistes.

So next week, dear, I shall be performing with professionals. It will certainly make a break for a few days and better than hanging around here doing nothing.

At the moment there is also talk of starting a full time divisional concert party and I believe the Div. is prepared to lay out quite a bit of money to start it. It's all very much in the air at the moment and I don't know whether to take the job on. To tell you the truth, darling, I haven't much interest in anything except getting back home to you. However, I may tackle it if they make the whole thing worthwhile ... I do hope that you will be able to get down to Brighton for Xmas and above all I hope that I shall be able to be with you my darling ...

Your ever loving husband,

Ray. x x x x x x

Lou and Al Roy. Fellow artistes with ENSA.

23.11.44.

My own darling wife,

... I promised in my last letter I would let you know how the E.N.S.A. show is going, so here goes.

We opened on Monday last for a week at a nearby theatre and everything was a huge success. It really is a smashing show darling and I wish you could see it. We have in the cast, Yvette Alain, (top line singing star, French of course), Lou and Al Roy (Continental Speciality Dancers from Brussels, Astaire-Rogers style), Stan King (Compère) and Sara Gregory (who is soon returning to England to play principal girl in the London Coliseum panto 'Goody Two Shoes'). I am playing with first class artistes, as you can guess dear. It's a very colourful show indeed and looks grand with bags of stage lighting.

I don't know how long the show will last, it all depends whether we can get permission from our commanding officer to carry on. As I mentioned in my previous letter, the Division is contemplating starting its own party, so we may get recalled to take part in it. The weather is terrible here, rain, rain and more rain, so I am only too glad to get away from army routine for a short while ...

I received a letter from Dad[16] *yesterday, everybody is keeping fine and his business is flourishing. He is advertising at three cinemas now and says it is bringing good results. Eddie is going on leave again soon. It appears that his mob draw for it and his name was first out of the hat ...*

Your ever loving husband, Ray. x x x x x x

P.S. The gloves are lovely and warm darling, 'just the job', R. x

16 Ray's father, Frank Harris

Yvette Alain. Fellow artiste with ENSA.

Ray's father had started a second-hand clothes business in Brighton since he had given up travelling around with his show. The letter Ray mentions is full of encouragement for his appearance with ENSA:

F.C. Harris,
Wardrobe Dealer,
4, St. Andrews Road, Brighton
(And at 1, Shaftesbury Rd., and Viaduct Rd.).

Wednesday
Nov 29th/44.

Dear Son,

We were glad to get your letter and to hear that you have been appearing with an E.N.S.A. show. You are definitely in good company and if I were you I should keep in touch with all of them, if possible, as you never know what it may lead to later on. If you could get on the Moss and Stoll tours you would be made. It would be a thousand times better than coming back to a dead-end job. You are evidently making some good contacts out there that should prove useful in the days to come.

Of course if you got on a good class tour you would want your own material, gags, songs, music and also band parts but these are easily got. Also it would be wise, once you have got a start to get in touch with a reliable agent. I shall be interested to hear how you are getting on both with E.N.S.A. and your own show. I am enclosing a little gag I heard the other day – not much but would fill a gap.

We all send our love to you.

All the best and cheerio,
Dad.

'I am surprised to hear you have still got some mud out there, I thought I had brought all that back with me last time.'

7911536. L/CPL HARRIS. R.
HQ SQUADRON, 7TH ARMOURED DIV
B.L.A.
23.11.44.

My own darling wife,
Many thanks once again for your last letter received O.K. also book, thanks a lot dear.
Well darling I promised in my last letter I would let you know how the ENSA show is going, so here goes.
We opened on Monday last for a week at a nearby theatre. + everything was a huge success. It really is a smashing show darling, + I wish you could see it. We have in the cast, Mdlle Yvette, Top-line singing star, French of course, Hal + Le Roy, Continental Speciality Dancers from Brussels (Astaire-Rogers style), Stan Kay compere, Sara Gregory, who is soon returning to England to play principal girl in the London

(2)
Coliseum panto "Goody Two Shoes"
I am playing with first class artistes as you can guess dear
Its a very colourful show, indeed and looks grand with bags of stage lighting.
I don't know how long the show will last, it all depends whether we can get permission from our commanding officer to carry on.
As I mentioned in my previous letter, the division is contemplating starting its own party, so we may get recalled to take part in it.
The weather is terrible here, rain rain + more rain, so I am only too glad to get away from army routine for a short while.
Things are very quiet now, nothing doing at all, I wonder how much longer it will be.
The days however seem to go a little quicker with the show, I think I should be really very depressed if I had nothing

Letter from Ray whilst performing with ENSA (23.11.1944).

27.11.44.

My own darling wife,

... Well darling the E.N.S.A. show has been a great success, so much so that I have been given permission to appear in it for a further week. Our own divisional show is very much in the air at the moment, but I have been told that I shall be producing it if it does come off. Still, as you say darling, I'm hoping that this so-and-so war will finish soon now and that army shows will be a thing of the past. If only the weather will keep fine, I feel sure that it can finish by Xmas.

We can get 48 hours leave into Brussels from where we are here, but as I am with the show, I don't think I shall trouble. In the first place, everything is really terribly expensive. In fact, to have a fairly quiet time there, some of our lads have been taking anything from £15 to £25. I think you will agree dear that it is far better to save the money until after the war, when we will be able to use it to a much better purpose.

Of course, Brussels is a very beautiful city ... The only trouble is that apart from everything being so dear, there are literally thousands of soldiers on leave daily, so wherever you go you still can't get away from uniform. I am certainly looking forward to the day darling when I hand in mine for good. Yes, I expect you are getting excited dear, with the prospects of getting back to Brighton soon ...

Your ever loving husband,
Ray. x x x x x x

29.11.44.

My own darling wife,

... We are playing a theatre in a small town near here for a couple of days and the show is going down very well indeed. I don't know what is going to happen next week. I suppose I shall have to go back and Miss Sara Gregory (Mrs. Stone) is returning to England to commence panto rehearsals at the London Coliseum.

I suppose the show will break up, a big pity, still there it is ...

All my love and kisses to you my dearest and God Bless.
Your ever loving husband,
Ray. x x x x x x

During the first week in December the Division was patrolling fields between Maesyck and Sittard across enemy defences and there was more action. Ray was back with the squadron on 4 December.

4.12.44.

My own darling wife,
Many thanks for your letters dear which were waiting for me on my return to the squadron today. Well darling the E.N.S.A. tour has finished and it was fun while it lasted.

We gave 22 shows in a fortnight altogether, so we didn't do so badly did we? The lads enjoyed it anyway. On returning back today, I saw my name on orders to attend a divisional concert party conference tomorrow morning at 9.30, so I will let you know the latest developments. At the moment our regimental sergeant-major isn't any too keen for me to get mixed up in any more concert party work. It appears that the corporal who took my job over while I have been away has made a real mess of the guard roll etc. The colonel seems very keen that I should be in the show, however, and I'm afraid that what he says goes. Anyway, we shall have to wait and see ...

It appears dear that leave to Blighty starts on Jan. 1st, so we have got something to look forward to. It's all very vague at the moment, but I think that there may be something in it. Rumour has it that it will be seven clear days.

Of course I was hoping it would be all over by then. Still it will be better than nothing won't it darling? ... I had another letter from Vera ... She is of course full of your going down to Brighton for good ...

Your ever loving husband,
Ray. x x x x x x

8.12.44.

My own darling wife,

... I have refused full time concert party work darling, for the time being, as I know I will stand a better chance of getting my leave quickly. Apart from this, I am not really keen on full time. I would much rather keep my squadron job and go out entertaining in my spare time. I am hoping that I shall get my seven days [leave] *fairly early in Jan.*

Won't it be wonderful dear? Of course, coming back out here won't be so good. Still it will break up the time we have been parted darling.

I have already posted you and everyone a Xmas card dear and I expect that you will get them rather early. The rain has set in again out here and conditions are getting very bad. Everything is literally swamped and nothing but mud everywhere. Of course, it is still possible for the war to end this year, but I am rather inclined to think that we shall have to wait until things dry up a bit. Still, by the time I have been home and back, it should be nearly finished ...

Must close now ... all my fondest love and kisses to you my darling and God Bless.

Your ever loving husband,

Ray. x x x x x x

Chapter 13

On Leave at Last

13.12.44.

My own darling,

... Well darling, I am certainly looking forward to the seven days leave. I just can't realize it somehow, after all it is nearly twelve months now isn't it? I am hoping to get away with the first bunch but don't know yet. In any case I don't suppose that I shall be able to let you know in time as we shall probably be here one day and away the next. That is why I do hope that you will be able to get down to Brighton so that I can come straight there to you ...

I am still on the orderly corporal's job, rushing around detailing chaps for guards, fatigues etc. On top of this I have been given the rationing returns for the unit to work out, so you can guess I am well occupied these days.

The weather is still pretty vile, bags of mud and everything pretty uncomfortable. It will certainly be wonderful to get away from it all for a week or so darling and we will make it a grand week ...

Your ever loving husband,
Ray. x x x x x x

On 16 December the Ardennes Offensive began when the Germans attacked the 40-mile front at Monschau (30 miles east of Liège).

On 19 December Ray was able to give Doreen a definite date for his leave.

19.12.44.

My own darling wife,

I am writing this letter to you hoping that you have managed to get down to Brighton by the time you receive it.

Well darling, I have got some good news as regards my leave. We were only allowed an allocation for 44 men for leave in January, so it was decided to draw names for the lucky places. Well 180 names went into the hat and there was a breathless hush while our commanding officer started to draw the slips. Imagine my surprise when the third slip out was L/Cpl Harris R.! Yes darling, I shall actually be leaving for home leave on Jan.7th. Of course, I don't know how long it will take me to reach England, but I should be home by the 9th.

I can hardly realize it yet. Something may crop up to alter it between now and the 7th, but I very much doubt it. The only thing is, of course, if they decide to cancel all leave. It would be just too bad but somehow I think everything will be O.K.

So keep your fingers crossed darling and look out for me round about the 9th! ...

Tell Vera I received the Christmas card O.K. and also the scripts from Dad, anyway I shall be able to thank them personally soon. What a grand time we are going to have darling and we are going to make the most of it ... love to all at No. 4 and all my love and kisses to you darling and God Bless.

Your ever loving husband,

Ray. x x x x x x

27.12.44.

My own darling wife,

... I am counting the hours until the 7th darling. I just can't believe that it's true. I shall be bringing a bit of cash with me so we shall have a really good time. We had a very quiet Xmas this year and a very sober one, so we shall have to make up for that.

I hope you are settling in O.K. darling. You can expect me on the 7th sometime. It may be a trifle late, I don't know yet. Still I shall come straight to Brighton as fast as I can, you can bet!

I don't think it will be much good writing any more letters after this one dear, as I shall be home by then.

Well darling, nothing much more this time, so I will close with all my fondest love and kisses and God Bless.

Your ever loving husband,
Ray. x x x x x x

A telegram confirms the letter on 30 December:

ARRIVING U.K. JAN 7th OR THEREABOUTS – LOVE RAY.

The 7th Armoured Division Christmas card, 1944.

Chapter 14

Advance into Germany

Ray arrived back at his unit on 17 January 1945.

17.1.45.

My own darling wife,

Just a few lines to say that I arrived at the unit safe and sound at four o'clock today. Well dear, it seems strange to be back once again. I felt very blue and miserable indeed on the way back, as you can guess. Still, I shan't ever be away so long again and that's some consolation isn't it darling? We did have a nice time while it lasted didn't we dear? Seven days soon goes though. It's not long enough really, still I am lucky being able to get my leave in first.

It was a miserable train journey back here, twelve hours and bitterly cold too. However, they looked after us as well as they could and dished us out a hot meal halfway back.

I was thinking of you all the time darling and wondering what you were doing. It seemed so strange that you were not with me. I have cheered up a bit now I'm back with the boys and am now looking forward to the next lot of leave. Super optimist eh?! ... The watch is still going strong and, as expected, I have received offers for it already, but nothing doing! I am hanging on to it! ... I hope D[17] *has fully recovered from the 'binge'. We shall have to have a good feed before our next one ... A million kisses dearest and God Bless you darling,*

17 Dorothy, Rex's wife

Your ever loving husband,
Ray. x x x x x x

P.S. I love you.

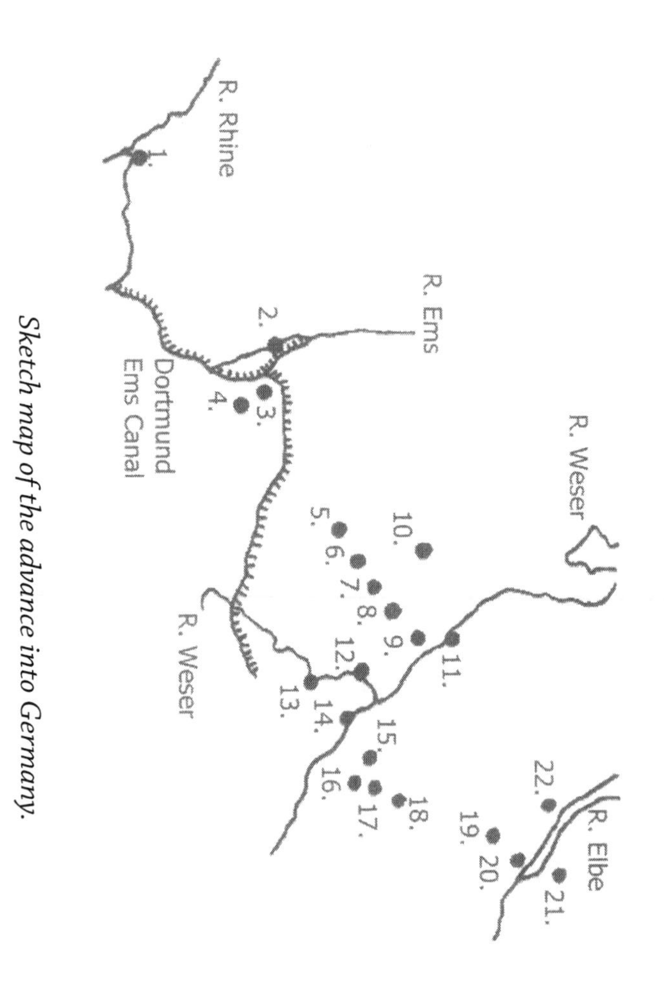

Sketch map of the advance into Germany.

1. Wesel
2. Rheine
3. Ibbenburen
4. Tecklenburg
5. Diepholz
6. Barnstorf
7. Twistringen
8. Bassum
9. Riede
10. Wildehausen
11. Bremen
12. Hoya
13. Nienburg
14. Rethem
15. Walsrode
16. Fallingbostel
17. Dorfmark
18. Soltau
19. Buchholz
20. Harburg
21. Buxtehude
22. Hamburg

By the time Ray got back, the next operation had started in freezing cold weather conditions bringing ice and snow. Before the advance to the Rhine could commence, the land between the River Maas and River Roer (the Roer Triangle) had to be taken from the enemy. This undertaking was known as 'Operation Blackcock'. It proved to be a very bitter conflict. The 7th Arm'd Div. (together with the 43rd and 52nd) were against two German divisions armed with 160 guns and defended by a dense barrier of mines.

The British tanks were painted white to blend in with the winter landscape. The icy weather in an area of fields filled with woods and ditches created hazardous driving conditions. After nine days of fierce combat from village to village the enemy was cleared from the area, which was held by the Division into February. Ray mentions the extreme weather in his next letter.

24.1.45.

My own darling wife,

... Well darling, I am settling in once again after my leave and it certainly takes a lot of getting used to after Brighton ... The local blokes were very pleased with the sixpences, in fact, one has made a tie pin out of one and it looks O.K. It has turned bitterly cold out here this last day or so and tonight it is below zero. You can guess how cold it really is, as I am wearing my overcoat at last. Ha! Ha! I've still got the sergeant major's shirt too. He hasn't asked for it yet, still I suppose I shall have to reluctantly hand it back to him. Roll on the day darling, when I am picking out my civvies suit, what do you say?

Two of the chaps who went on leave with me haven't come back yet and are now posted as deserters. It's not worth it, as well as not playing the game with the lads here who are waiting for leave. I expect they will catch it very hot when they get them.

Well my darling, I am missing you so much now, still it can't last much longer and our days of being apart are numbered. Won't it be wonderful when I am home for good and no more goodbyes? We can really start living then can't we darling? Well sweet, I shall have to close once again. There's not much news to tell you except I love you darling with all my heart. You know that don't you dear? I shan't really be happy until I am with you for always.

Goodnight dear, all my fondest love and kisses and God Bless.

Your ever loving husband,
Ray. x x x x x x

The next letter reveals that Doreen is staying with Ray's friends Rex, Dorothy and their little girl Joan at 3 Albert Road, Brighton.

30.1.45.

My own darling wife,
... I'm glad that you are settling in O.K. with Rex and D ...

31.1.45.

My own darling wife,
... Well darling the news is certainly sensational isn't it? At the time of writing the Russians are only 65 miles off Berlin. It doesn't seem possible ... I am still acting orderly sergeant and have been pretty busy these last two days. I have had to look after a prisoner, a deserter who has just been picked up. The future is not very bright for him, as after the Court Martial, he forfeits all his foreign service and starts again as a 'rookie' which means he will be more or less a cert. for Burma. It certainly pays to keep your nose clean in the army just now.

At the moment I am billeted in our squadron canteen, not too comfortable, but very warm and that's the main thing. We have got plenty of books and a wireless, so we are not too badly off. I expected to hear Donald Peers' broadcast in 'Variety Bandbox' (he was advertised to do so) but he didn't come on, must have been indisposed. Our chaps are still going on leave, a few at a time. Some of them won't be going until June or July, so you can guess darling, how lucky I was. I am missing you so much darling ...

Your ever loving husband,
Ray. x x x x x x

P.S. Give Rex, D. and Joan my fondest regards dear.

On 6 February the British troops (under Canadian command) attacked through the Reichswald into the south in order to clear the left bank of the Rhine. The Americans attacked in the north so that they could meet up with them. There was harsh fighting in terrible weather until 10 March. On 7 March, however, the Americans took Cologne and a few days later, the whole of the west bank of the Rhine was cleared.

A letter dated 7 February 1945 mentions the fact that Doreen now has a part-time job in Brighton and that Ray will receive £100 in war gratuities. The weather has changed. Ray writes:

...it's very bad since the thaw. Everything is a sea of mud and to crown it all, it has started to rain heavily. Roll on the day darling when we can sit by our own fire, just you and I and just look back on all this ...

On 11 February 1945 Ray writes from the squadron canteen:

... it's fairly empty at the moment, two chaps playing a rather half hearted game of darts and one bloke reading. Everybody is getting a little war weary now which is only to be expected as this mob has been on the go almost continuously since 1940 and that's five years! ...

As well as looking backwards, Ray is obviously, in the next letter, starting to plan for his future with Doreen.

14.2.45.

My own darling wife,

... I see in the papers darling that they are still going to manufacture utility furniture after the war. That's not so good is it dear? I expect the real stuff is going to be pretty expensive don't you?

Have you any idea how much Rex paid for all his? I know he has got it on the instalment system. I don't fancy that somehow do you darling? ... With a bit of luck we should have about £200 saved up with my gratuity ... Won't it be grand when we have our own little place darling? Just you and me. It's the one day I'm praying for ... As Vera mentioned in her last letter, we are going to have some grand times all together, especially summer days. I know it won't take long for us to forget these long years we have been apart my darling. Just fancy dear, it's nearly twelve months since we were married ...

On 19 February 1945 Ray sends greetings for his and Doreen's first wedding anniversary.

... I do hope you receive the letter by the 26th and all my fondest love darling for our Wedding Anniversary ... A really big X for the 26th darling ...

On 21 February the 7th Arm'd Div. was taken from the line, away from the action, in order to undergo training at Bree and Weert. It was being prepared for 'Operation Plunder', the crossing of the Rhine.

24.2.45.

My own darling wife,

... I don't know how you feel about it dear, but after giving it serious thought, I suggest we wait until I get out of the army before we buy anything ... I will send what I save home to you darling to put in the bank.

... I wouldn't like to start buying anything now and then find

out later we could have afforded to buy something better ... Well darling, the weather has brightened up a bit these last few days. Spring appears to be a little early this year. News is still good, although this Hun can certainly seem to take it. I wonder how long he can keep it up? Still the end can come at any time now. A couple of months should see it through. I know I shan't be able to realize it when it does come darling. How much it will mean to us both dear and millions like us. My old civilian days seem to be a part of another life. How long ago it all seems doesn't it darling?

I just do my work mechanically these days waiting for the end. I have just been given another job now, gunnery instructor for a fortnight ...

More details of the training in this period of the war are revealed in the next letter.

28.2.45.

My own darling wife,

... I am terribly busy these days as we are undergoing a spell of hectic training. What with doing acting orderly sergeant as well, I am on the go all day. Tomorrow, for instance, I am instructing on gunnery at 9 a.m. From there I go on to the foot drill, then a lecture and carry on to P.T. I also have to detail all the guards and see they are O.K. and work out ration strengths. So you can guess I don't get a lot of time for myself.

Well darling, I hope you have received my last letter about the furniture etc. Of course, if you would rather get it before I get home, do so by all means but I wouldn't like to rush things. After all it is a very important thing our future home isn't it darling? I am so keen to have it as nice as possible. I shall be anxious to hear what you think about it all dear.

The news still keeps pretty good doesn't it? I think the end will come just when we are not expecting it ... I don't know how long my letters take to reach you dear, but I think I had better wish you many happy returns for your birthday ... we are so out in the wilds here I can't get a thing. I had great hopes of getting 48 hours leave in Brussels but they have cancelled that now ...

A million kisses dear and God Bless. Goodnight Sweetheart,

Your ever loving husband,

Ray. x x x x x x

The next letter (3 March 1945) reveals that Eddie is leaving the RAF and is about to go into the army but on an optimistic note Ray writes:

I think the end is near. I see by the papers that all the demobilization centres have got to be ready by 1st April, so I should imagine that's a pointer shouldn't you?

... although it is pretty cold, the rain keeps off and we are getting quite a bit of sunshine. There's one thing we have got the better weather in front of us now and it won't be long before the Summer comes along and with it peace I hope.

Without being unduly optimistic I am counting on being out of the Army by October or November this year. I am definitely looking forward to my first Xmas at home for five years and I hope I shan't be disappointed. Fancy taking Sunday School classes darling!

In the next letter (9 March 1945) Ray writes that he:

Happened to be passing a small shop in the village where we are at the moment and to my surprise I spotted a Birthday card, an English one too so I bought it and sent it off to you darling ...

Spring seems to have arrived to stay ... It all seems to make peace very near which I am sure it is. Anyway whether it rains snows or shines on that day it will be a June day for us both won't it darling?

In a letter dated 12 March 1945 Ray writes:

The Rhine crossing was a bit of good news wasn't it? It has definitely speeded up the end.

The next (19 March 1945) expresses the hope that Eddie:

... doesn't have to go out East. He shouldn't do as he has as much service as me, five years in June and he is nearly 29. That puts him in round about 25 or 26 group. He may, however, be called upon for army of occupation out here for a few months ... Will you let me have his address darling? ... I am having a bit of trouble again with my teeth. I keep dosing myself with aspirins but suppose it will all end with the inevitable visit to the dentist. What a Life!

On 27 March Ray's division also crossed the Rhine at Wesel and then began the advance towards Rheine where an enemy airfield was situated. On the same day Ray wrote again to Doreen.

27.3.45.

My own darling wife,

Once again many thanks dear for your letters all of which I have received O.K. I'm afraid I haven't been able to write as frequently lately, but what with the recent turn of events I know that you will understand darling ...

He also reveals that he has had some dental treatment and has written to Eddie and then concludes:

... I feel that being with this Division with its long record of fighting service in the field is an advantage and may get a little priority in the demobilization. I miss you so much darling, but the end of the road is in sight ...

Your ever loving husband,

Ray. xxxxxx

During this stage of the war there were many different actions being performed at the same time by various groups in each division. Enemy opposition was encountered all the way. It was often necessary to target the enemy with machine gun fire from the tanks as bazookas were used. The divisions' training in such warfare (mentioned by Ray in previous letters) means they were well prepared. As they travelled through each village it had to be cleared. Bridges that had been blown up had to be rebuilt and roads opened to keep the advance moving swiftly. All these operations were strongly supported by the tanks.

Ray, in a letter dated 31 March 1945, says:

> *I suppose you have heard the old 7th Armoured mentioned a few times lately ... we are always on the move these days ...*
>
> *A lot of our chaps have been a bit off colour lately, especially the old desert campaigners. I think they are all just a little war weary now, which is only to be expected when you think of the record of the old Desert Rats ... Goodnight darling ...*

On 1 April the advance into Rheine was successfully manoeuvred. All the bridges over the Ems were blown and opposition was fierce but, by 2 April, Rheine was cleared of the enemy. By this time the Dortmund–Ems Canal had also been crossed and Tecklenburg taken. The advance continued to Ibbenbüren. The Germans were finally overthrown as the town was reduced to flames.

A bridge was captured over the Weser–Ems Canal and the march continued towards Diepholz where there was a sudden, surprise attack by the German air force.

The River Weser was crossed on 5 April. Hoya (40 miles from Diepholz) was reached before dawn on 6 April. Unable to cross the bridges the Division turned north in order to cut off the Germans retreating from Bremen.

7.4.45.

My own darling wife,

Just a few lines to let you know that I'm O.K. ... I suppose that you have heard on the wireless and in the papers that the old 7th is once more leading the field ... We are on the go day and night just like the early days in Belgium and Holland, in fact we are standing by now to move once again. If you don't hear from me quite so often, please <u>don't worry darling</u>, as I am quite O.K. We are all looking forward to a speedy end now. It should finish by the end of the month ...

The weather is clearing up a bit now after a fortnight of rain, which didn't make things any too pleasant as we are camping in the open once more. Well darling, please excuse this very hasty letter but am really in a terrible hurry to get it off. Will write a longer one when I can get a couple of hours although Lord knows when that will be ... All my fondest love and kisses, God Bless,

Your ever loving husband,

Ray. x x x x x x

The next day, after a further bitter struggle, Twistringen and Bassum were taken. Barnstorf and Riede followed and by 10 April Wildeshausen was occupied. However, the Germans sneaked into the town and four tanks were destroyed.

By this time, it was clear that the taking of Bremen would be an extremely arduous undertaking and unsuitable for an armoured division to tackle. At this point, therefore, the 3rd Division took over and Ray's division was moved southeast to Nienburg. On the same day (10 April) Ray sent another letter enclosing £4, which he won in the squadron football sweep, and the next day the Division entered Rethem.

In the next letter, Ray is able to write at length.

14.4.45.

My own darling wife,

At last I can settle down and write a reasonably long letter. As you know dear we have been travelling very fast this week or so. It has been impossible to sit down and write. Well darling, things are O.K. and everything has been going grand. The old 'Desert Rats' certainly set a hot pace for everybody and it is a well known fact that we have played a big part in the final victory bid.

In spite of everything I suppose that I am really glad deep down that I didn't miss it and I get a little self satisfaction in knowing that I started with the old 7th in the early days and have seen every campaign with them.

As you know, we are well in Germany now and the scene changes every hour. One minute you are racing through towns that are literally ruins, and the next, through places absolutely untouched. The people seem dazed with it all, especially when they see the masses of vehicles, guns, planes and equipment Hitler appears to have told them we hadn't got. The non-fraternization order however is very strict and we are not allowed to have anything to do with the German people and that's O.K. by me.

The country is really very beautiful and, with the grand weather we are having, makes one feel a little homesick. Still, altogether darling, it is quite an experience and a lot different from the long drawn out years on the desert.

Of course we are all wondering when V.E. Day will be announced. Personally, I think very soon now and, in any case, before 1st June.

Various rumours are going around in regards to demobbing. Some say that No. 1 to 4 groups are being demobbed this month (I read this in 'The Empire Sunday News'). Two months after this, 6 to 20 groups and then a group a month. If this is right, Dec. should see me out, but of course, it is all rumours and there is nothing really official yet. If they don't bring this five years scheme down to four and a half for overseas service, I shan't get my thirty days leave until the end of Dec. Still that should come in with 56 days (which everybody gets) and another 60 days (1 day for every month abroad) so altogether I should qualify for 146 days with full pay round about the end of the year. Not bad eh darling if it comes off!

It's all I think about sweetheart, getting back to you. I miss you so much darling and love you so much. I know I shall never really be content until I'm with you again.

We are going to be so happy dear and we have so much to look forward to, planning our home and settling down for the years to come. Maybe they won't all be sunny days and perhaps a few rainy ones will creep in ... as long as we are together rain or shine will be O.K. ... meanwhile all my love darling, a million kisses and God Bless,

Your ever loving husband,

Ray. x x x x x x

P.S. Love and regards to Rex, De and Joan and tell them it won't be long now.

From 15 April to 7 May, the Division was moving forward to the Elbe at Harburg in order to cut off the motorway between Bremen and Hamburg which was used by the Germans.

7911536. L/CPL. HARRIS. R.
HQ SQUADRON, 7TH ARMOURED DIV.
B.L.A.
14.4.45.

My own darling wife,
At last I can settle down & write a reasonably long letter.
As you know dear we have been travelling very fast this last week or so, & it has been impossible to sit down & write.
Well darling things are OK & everything has been going grand. The old Desert Rats certainly set a hot pace for everybody, & it is a well-known fact that we have played a big part in the

(2)

final victory bid.
In spite of everything I suppose that I am really glad deep down that I didn't miss it, & I get a little self satisfaction in knowing that I started with the old 7TH in the early days & have seen every campaign with them.
As you know we are well in Germany now, & the scene changes every hour. One minute you are racing through towns that are literally ruins, & the next, through places absolutely untouched. The people seem dazed with it all, especially when they see the masses of vehicles, guns, planes & equipment which

(3)

Hitler appears to have told them we hadn't got.
The non-fraternization order however is very strict, & we are not allowed to have anything to do with the German people and that's OK by me.
The country is really very beautiful & with the grand weather we are having, makes one feel a little homesick.
Still, altogether darling it is quite an experience & a lot different from the long drawn out years on the desert.
Of course, we are all wondering when V DAY will be announced.
Personally I think very soon now, and in any case before June 1st. Various rumours are

One of Ray's letters during the advance into Germany (14.04.1945), pages 1–3.

(4)

going around in regards to
demobbing. Some say that no1
to 5 groups are being demobbed
this month (I read this in the
Empire Sunday News), + two months
after this finishes out here 5 to
20 groups + then a group a
month. If this is right, Dec
should see me out, but of
course it is all rumours +
there is nothing really official
yet. If they don't bring this
five years scheme down to four-
and a half for over seas service
I shant get my thirty days
leave until the end of Dec.
still, that should come in
with 56 days (which everybody
gets) and another 60 days (1 day
for every month abroad) so al-

(5)

-together I should qualify
for 146 days with full pay
round about the end of the
year, not bad eh! darling!
if it comes off.
Its all I think about sweet-
-heart, getting back to you
I miss you so much darling,
+ love you so much. I know
I shall never really be content
until I'm with you again.
We are going to be so happy
dear. + we have so much to
look forward to, planning our
home + settling down for the
years to come.
Maybe, they may not all be
sunny days and perhaps a
few rainy ones will creep in
but we both know from our

(6)

own family lives what they are,
+ as long as we are together
rain or shine we'll be OK.
I hope you received the £4
in postal orders alright dear.
a bit of luck wasn't it darling.
Well sweetheart. I think that's
all the news for this time
I will write again as soon as
possible, meanwhile all my love
darling, a million Kisses +
God Bless

Your ever loving husband
Ray

P.S Love + regards to Rex Dc +
Joan + tell them it won't be
long now R.

NATIONAL WAR EFFORT. PLEASE USE BOTH SIDES OF PAPER

One of Ray's letters during the advance into Germany (14.04.1945), pages 4–6.

The area between Soltau and Harburg had to be cleared before Hamburg could finally be taken. Fighting continued in every town and village on every route that the Allies took. On 15 April the Rethem bridgehead was crossed and Walsrode was occupied. All the roads were in a pitiful state with large holes where the Germans had bombed them.

The Division advanced in two groups, one towards Soltau and the other to the north. Roads blocked by fallen trees, mines and booby traps and ruined bridges had to be negotiated but by 16 April the Division was only two miles from Soltau. Further north, Fallingbostel was held and Dorfmark reached by nightfall.

On 16 April the Division liberated a prisoner of war camp at Fallingbostel. Some of the prisoners were from the 7th Arm'd Div., captured by the enemy in the desert. Many were completely overcome with emotion and, unable to speak, could only shake hands with their liberators. Many thousands of British and Americans had been waiting five years to be released.

It was about this time that the concentration camp at Belsen was surrendered. Between 40,000 and 60,000 political prisoners were found in the most horrific conditions imaginable.

By 17 April Soltau was cleared and the Division took bridges over the Elbe at Harburg. On 18 April, Tostedt was taken, on 19 April Buchholz and, by this time, Bremen. The Division now had two aims:

(1) To cut off the motorway between Bremen and Hamburg and then capture Harburg.

(2) To defeat the enemy in the forests north of Soltau, a difficult task as the Germans were still well equipped in this area.

On 19 April, part of the first aim was achieved as the motorway was cut off. On the same day, Ray writes again.

19.4.45.

My own darling wife,

... We are still travelling fast ... Churchill makes a speech today and I am hoping he will tell us a thing or two. All the papers seem very optimistic don't they? I am rather inclined to think they overdo it at times. Yes, it was a great pity about Roosevelt,[18] *just at this stage of the war too. A great shame he couldn't live to see the end ...*

I see in the papers that they are issuing a booklet called 'Release and Pre Release' to the forces. I am looking forward to reading one of these, as I understand it gives you some idea how the demobbing works out ...

We had a mobile cinema a couple of weeks back. They showed two films, Deanna Durbin in 'White Christmas' which was very good and I enjoyed it very much. The other film, Tommy Trinder in 'Champagne Charlie', was terrible, in fact, the lads gave it the 'bird'. The films have got to be up to standard out here, as the shows are nearly always given in an old barn, so the seating accommodation isn't exactly comfortable. The film has got to be good, otherwise the chaps are apt to get a little restless and once that happens you may as well as finish there and then. Still, we enjoy most of the films and it certainly makes a break ... We will be moving again anytime now so I will conclude with all my fondest love darling, a million kisses and God Bless,

Your ever loving husband,

Ray. x x x x x x

By 20 April there was much shelling around Harburg as the Germans vigorously defended it and by 21 April the only remaining bridge over the Elbe was destroyed, preventing Harburg from being entered. The same day, Buxtehude

18 The president of the USA, who had died a week earlier

surrendered. By this time the Baltic Sea had been reached and Holland was to be liberated soon afterwards. Not only had the Russians penetrated Berlin but the Americans had broken through the enemy front in Czechoslovakia and Bavaria. The war was in the last stages.

The 7th Arm'd Div. now concentrated on ridding the areas south and southwest of Harburg of what was left of the enemy. Many prisoners were taken near Soltau.

In Ray's next letter he responds to Doreen's suggestion that they share Rex and Dorothy's house when he leaves the army. They did in fact eventually rent the flat beneath them at 3 Albert Road, Brighton.

22.4.45.

My own darling wife,

... I think it would be a very good idea to share a house with Rex and De if it could be arranged ... The general news is very good at the moment, dear. One of the lads has just come along to say that the Russians are in the suburbs of Berlin. It can't possibly last much longer. The weather has changed a bit this last couple of days and we are getting a drop of rain. Still we can't grumble as it has been fine nearly every day since we crossed the Rhine.

We have been liberating quite a few P.O.W. camps lately and have come across some of the old 'Desert Rats' who were captured in the early days in the desert. They certainly were glad to see us. I was speaking to an R.A.F. pilot whom we released a couple of days ago. He claimed to be the oldest prisoner of war out here.

It seems that he was in the very first raid on Germany on 3/4th September 1939. He was shot down and had been a prisoner ever since, so he's had quite a spell behind barbed wire and a pretty rough time as well I believe ... All my fondest love and a million kisses, God Bless.

Your ever loving husband,

Ray. x x x x x x

26.4.45.

My own darling wife,

... Yesterday we had our demob. group numbers entered into our pay books and signed by an officer ... Berlin certainly seems to be getting a bashing. I hope Jerry isn't going to make a nuisance of himself defending these pockets of resistance, otherwise I'm afraid it's going to be rather a long drawn out affair. I can't understand why he hasn't packed in. Still the end is bound to come darling, probably just when we are not expecting it.

The days are dragging a bit now, roll on my next leave!

Of course we are not allowed out much now we are in Germany and all towns are strictly out of bounds ...

Your ever loving husband,
Ray. x x x x x x

Chapter 15

The Surrender of Hamburg

By the end of April there were rumours of (1) the surrender of Germany, (2) Hitler's plan to make one last stand against the Allies in Berlin and (3) the desertion of German leaders.

On 29 April, two German officers and a civilian, bearing a white flag, arrived at divisional headquarters. This event resulted in General Lyne writing to General Wolz demanding that Hamburg surrender. He stated that if this demand wasn't met, there would be another air raid.

On the same day Ray writes at length.

29.4.45.

My own darling wife,

Just a few more lines once again dear. Well darling it's Sunday evening, and I am sitting in the front of a 3 ton lorry writing this letter.

It is raining pretty hard at the moment and bitterly cold, in fact it reminds me of that well known song 'Oh What a Lovely Way to Spend an Evening' and especially on a Sunday!

Still we are all looking forward now very optimistically to the end, probably due to the fact that the news has just come through that Mussolini has been hung. Yes darling, I don't think it will be long now until I am spending all my Sunday evenings with you.

Later on tonight we are having a bit of a sing song. We have managed to borrow (?) a German piano together with a few bottles of wine. So round about 10 o'clock tonight I shall probably be giving a couple of requests: 'Buddy Can You Spare a Dime?' and 'Rolling Along'. We shall have Ronnie Vaughan (an ex 'Jerboa Stroller', you will probably remember me telling you about him darling) on the piano. We don't get much in the way of entertainment, so have to provide our own, anyway the lads enjoy it and it keeps their minds off the war a bit.

Yes, I shall be looking forward to hearing the Inkspots singing 'Whispering Grass' they are very good.

By the way darling there is something else you can get for me (I bet you think I'm a nuisance) if you could manage it. I have been getting a terrible lot of dandruff lately. I keep washing my hair, but it's no good. Well darling what I want is a bottle of <u>Pure</u> Silvikrin which I think you can get at Boots along the London Road. It's pretty dear about 10/6 I believe, but all our chaps are sending home for it and I really would like some if you can manage it. Just ask for <u>Pure</u> Silvikrin (sounds like an advert doesn't it?) only they may give you the lotion which isn't so good. I should be very grateful darling if you could get some for me only you would be surprised how very little we can get out here.

I haven't drawn a penny since I came on leave in Jan., so the old credits must be up to something like £25 once again. Money means nothing in this country, so I don't draw any ...

I could write forever on how much I love you darling and how I long to be back again, you know that don't you darling? I know we are both trying to be so patient and keeping our chins up. We have been doing it for so long now, that I'm sure that Lady Luck will soon be with us both again and we shall have one another for always.

Goodnight my darling, a million kisses and God Bless.

Your loving husband,

Ray. x x x x x x

On 1 May General Wolz agreed that Hamburg would surrender within 48 hours and, at the same time, the news broke that Hitler was dead.

General Wolz arrived at divisional headquarters on 2 May to discuss the surrender. The next day Admiral Doenitz took over from Hitler as head of state and the 7th Arm'd Div. passed through the dock area. On 4 May, thousands of Germans surrendered and on 5 May all fighting ended by 8 a.m.

6.5.45.

My own darling wife,
Just a few lines in haste while I have a few minutes to spare ... As you know the Div is moving fast again and my time is very limited. Well dear, the end is very near now and the blue sky is just appearing. I know I shan't realize it when V.E. Day is announced. The weather has turned nasty again but who cares?

I heard from a very old friend of mine today, Jimmie Parker (late of 'The Strollers'), who is in the military police in London. He enclosed a very old photo of me working a double act near Tobruk nearly three years ago ... we are moving on any minute ... fondest love sweetheart and a million kisses. Goodnight dear.

Your ever loving husband,
Ray. x x x x x x

The Germans continued to be relieved of their arms and the Division moved on to Kiel Canal (45 miles northwest of Hamburg). There 10,000 sailors gave themselves up.

VE Day was celebrated on 8 May amidst rejoicing. Bonfires were lit and Churchill made a speech at divisional headquarters where there was a short service of thanksgiving.

9.5.45.

My own darling wife,
Well! It's all over at last dear and I can't realize it can you?

After all these long years of waiting and hoping, it's finished! It's a wonderful thought to know that I can now look forward to getting home darling. Funnily enough, when we heard the great news, (we knew some time before the papers announced it), nobody seemed unduly excited. I suppose this was because it has been so long and everybody more or less expected it. We celebrated in real style last night, however, and had a private war of our own. There were revolvers, automatics, sten guns, brens and ack ack going off all over the place. It's a miracle to me that nobody got shot up. The boys just went mad, helped along of course by bags of booze. Personally, I turned in early. I didn't fancy a bullet through the nut at this stage. Still, the lads enjoyed it all and nobody was any the worse off this morning except, of course, the inevitable 'hangovers' ...

I haven't heard anything else about leave yet, but should be O.K. round about June. I wonder how they will work the demobbing. I am hoping to be out by Xmas. We shall probably hang on out here in occupation for some time, but, of course, nobody knows anything yet ...

Your ever loving husband,
Ray. x x x x x x

PLEASE ADDRESS YOUR REPLY TO
Y.M.C.A.
No 7911536. Rank L/CPL.
Name HARRIS. R.
Address HQ SQUADRON, 7TH ARMOURED DIVISION B.L.A.
Date 9.5.45.
My own darling wife,
Well! its all over at last dear, & I can't realize it, can you?
After all these long years of waiting & hoping, its finished!
It's a wonderful thought to know that I can now look for-ward to getting home darling.
Funnily enough, when we heard the great news (We knew some time before the papers announced it) nobody seemed unduly excited.
I suppose this was because it has been so long, & everybody more or less expected it.
We celebrated in real style last night however, & had a private war of our own.
There were revolvers, automatics
NATIONAL WAR EFFORT. PLEASE USE BOTH SIDES OF PAPER

PLEASE ADDRESS YOUR REPLY TO
Y.M.C.A.
No. Rank
Name
Address
Date
(2)
sten guns, brens, & ack ack going off all over the place. Its a miracle to me that nobody got shot up. The boys just went mad, helped along of course, by bags of booze.
Personally, I turned in early.
I didn't fancy a bullet through the nut at this stage.
Still, the lads enjoyed it all, and nobody was any the worse off this morning, except of course the inevitable 'hangovers'.
Well darling, I had another bit of luck again last week end, what do you think? I won the football sweep again. Can you beat it!
So shall be sending another £5 home, look out for it.
NATIONAL WAR EFFORT. PLEASE USE BOTH SIDES OF PAPER

Ray's letter written the day after VE Day (09.05.1945).

10.5.45.

My own darling wife,
... I suppose Brighton made whoopee on V.E. Day didn't they? I do wish that I could have been there ... We have already started spit and polish parades etc., and I'm none too keen at this stage. Even now I can't seem to realize that the war is really over out here and I know it won't come home to me until I am back with you darling.

All the boys are anxiously waiting for something official about demobbing and it's all they talk about now ...

I know we are going to be so happy sweetheart and make up for all this long time apart. It is going to be a rather boring time for me now until I get out and the days are dragging a bit already.

Your ever loving husband,
Ray.

A big V.E. X from me darling.

16.5.45.

My own darling wife,
... The weather has been beautiful this last few weeks, real Victory weather ... We are almost back to peace time soldiering now, bags of parades and a general tightening up of discipline all round ...

24.5.45.

... did you see in the papers about war ribbons? It appears that I qualify for about four. The African Star (which I have already). The 1939–45 Star. The Italian Star and the French and German Star, quite an assortment of colours. Still they are really not of any great importance. All I want is to get back to you darling, for always ... We are getting bags of parades now. By the way darling, I wonder if you could send me some metal polish, as we have quite a lot of brass on our equipment and I just can't get anything to clean it with. Also a tin of Kiwi black boot polish

if you could manage it. We are fairly comfortable in rooms of our own at the moment. I have a nice little place with bed, wash basin, electric light and a beautiful Philips radio ...

Sometimes I think how lucky I have been through four years of active service ... lots of our lads who fell in the desert, in Italy and over here will not come back ... I think Fate has been very kind and a few months of waiting until I get back to you darling is really nothing ...

A million kisses,

Your ever loving husband,

Ray. x x x x x x

Chapter 16

Occupation and Leave

29.5.45.

My own darling wife,

... according to reliable reports I should be out in Nov. and I am really counting the days until then. At the moment, we are not too badly off in civilian houses having moved to another town since I last wrote, anyway, I'll never be content until I am back again with you sweetheart, and it's the only day I live for ...

I may be back in concert party work again in a week or so. Now that the war is over, I feel that I should be doing a better job of work in entertaining than walking around with a notebook and pencil detailing chaps for fatigues. After all, entertainment is very important out here now as the lads are getting a little impatient until their demob. group comes up ...

There is no need for me to tell you darling how much I am yearning to be with you once again and to hold you in my arms and tell you how much I love you and have missed you. Thank God our days of being apart are numbered and it won't be long now until we are together for always and always.

What an age of waiting it has seemed hasn't it? I don't think I could stand much longer of it, being away so long from somebody I love so much. Still dearest, as we have both said time and time again, we will really and truly make up for it soon now. Meanwhile we will both be counting the weeks to that day, our V.E. Day, when all the dreams we have built up through these last few years come true. I know darling, when that day does come and it's not far off, we will both say that it certainly has been worth waiting for.

Well sweetheart, I shall have to close once again with all my fondest love and kisses. Goodnight dear and God Bless,

Your ever loving husband,

Ray. x x x x x x

P.S. Love and regards to all at No. 3.

Ray, Germany 1945.

For many months after Germany's surrender, the 7th Arm'd Div. became the army of occupation stretching across an area of 80 miles, from Hamburg to the Danish frontier. It became responsible for the organisation of thousands of German prisoners, refugees and displaced Eastern Europeans.

In Ray's next letter, dated 4 June 1945, he says,

We have now settled down to peacetime soldiering, which isn't too bad, once you have got all your equipment cleaned up. We only have one spit and polish parade a week, on Saturday mornings, so we can't grouse.

6.6.45.

... Well darling, I'm sitting in my room with the radio on playing some very sentimental music and I must confess that I am feeling just a little blue. I do so long to be with you again darling and I know that this last wait is going to be the hardest of all. I have just come back from the squadron canteen, and have been trying to cheer the lads up a bit (they are all pretty well browned off) with a few gags ...

I still haven't drawn any pay since Jan. 5th and should have over £40 in credit ...

Your ever loving husband,
Ray. x x x x x x

P.S. Did I remember to tell you how much I love you darling? Goodnight sweetheart.

In a letter dated 9 June 1945 Ray tells Doreen,

I have heard ... news about the repatriation scheme, that is overseas service. It appears that they have lowered it from five years to four years. As I have already done four and a half, I should be hearing about this very soon. I'm certainly looking forward to something in the way of leave very soon now darling...

In the next letter (14 June 1945) Ray mentions the photo he has sent home of his performance at Tobruk.

I shall always remember that particular performance as early the next morning, there was a big flap on and Jerry was just about to come right through our lines, which he did do. It wasn't long before we found ourselves right back to Alamein and nearly into Alexandria. Those were the days! Still I wouldn't have them back for a pension. Exactly five years yesterday I joined the army, quite an old soldier now darling. I never forget that day when poor old Eddie, Vera and myself walked up to Brighton Station ...

In the next letter (17 June 1945) Ray tells Doreen he has come across an album of stamps, some of which are over a hundred years old, and asks if she will send him a foreign stamp catalogue. He also reveals that he is about to start a new job as post corporal in charge of all the mail. The first groups of men (1–11) were being demobbed the next day (18 June).

After announcing that he is getting his teeth thoroughly overhauled in time for 'Civvie Street' Ray adds a postscript:

P.S. If you can't get a stamp price catalogue from Smith's darling, you will probably get one from one of the old bookshops in the Lanes, if you happen to be down that way. What a man this Harris merchant is! First, it's metal polish! Boot polish! Hair tonic! Brighton and Hove Heralds! and now foreign stamps! It's a good job you understand me darling. I'm all out for making a few quid while the going is good and there's nothing like turning a few stamps into a suite of furniture eh darling!

Goodnight sweet!
I love you,
R. xxxxxx

A very brief letter written the next day (18 June 1945) states that Doreen need not bother about the catalogue after all, as he is having the stamps valued in Germany. He has also heard that his leave has been granted for the first week in July.

21.6.45.

My own darling wife,

... Sorry I haven't written for the last day or so, but to tell you the truth I have been up to my neck in work with this new post job. Well darling, if everything goes O.K., I should be in England by the 5th of July, that is a fortnight today. I do hope that nothing crops up in the meantime, but I don't see why it should, although we are very short staffed at the moment and the problem is getting people to fill the jobs ... I am counting the days until I see you again dearest. I know that I shan't realize it until I am holding you in my arms again darling.

By the way dearest, you will see there is a slight change in my address now, so in future please put: Rear H.Q. Squadron, otherwise your letters may go to our main squadron and they are some distance from here ... We have to leave the unit three or four days before our leave day so that means I shall be away from here round about the 1st or 2nd of July. We get 11 days now and my month's leave shouldn't be far off now, so everything looks very rosy for us darling ...

23.6.45.

... all being well I shall be home on the 5th July. I have just seen our squadron leave list for July and my name is down for that date, so that's good enough for me. The only thing that can delay me now is bad sailing weather, and if the weather keeps like it is at the moment, there's not much danger of that.

Well darling, there's no need for me to tell you how much I am longing for the 5th to come along and I'm patiently counting the days until then ...

25.6.45.

... Well darling a week today, I should be on the way home. I can hardly believe it. By the way I shall probably be a little late arriving on the 5th dear (remember last time?) so I wonder whether you could get two or three bottles of beer in for a little home coming drink. I do hope the weather will be kind to us dear and the rain keeps off, still, whatever the weather, the main thing is that I shall be home with you darling ... By the way, I shall come around to No. 3 is that O.K. dear? Please let me know ...

Please give everybody my love and regards and tell them I shall be seeing them very soon now. Goodnight sweetheart.

Your ever loving husband,

Ray. x x x x x x

P.S. I shall be collecting a few of these soon now darling. R. x x x x x x

Chapter 17

Berlin and More Leave

After Ray's leave, his next letter was written from Berlin, where a triumphant victory parade was being planned for 21 July.

7911 536 L/CPL HARRIS R.
H.Q. BRITISH TROOPS,
BERLIN.

20.7.45.

My own darling wife,

... As you can see I have landed up in Berlin after all and what a journey I have had getting here since I left you on Monday. We landed up at Folkestone going back at about 12 o/c noon and were then taken to Connaught Barracks there to spend the night as the day's sailing was cancelled after all.

We all could have had an extra day's leave at home if they had let us know in time. Just my luck and just like the army! Well, we sailed the next day to Calais and started the long weary train journey to Hamburg at about 10 o/c at night. After 36 hours on the train we eventually arrived. From there we did another 50 miles to where I left the squadron. When we got there we found they had moved to Berlin 290 miles away. Can you beat it?

This was about 10 o/c yesterday morning, so we had to get on another lorry and start for Berlin. We arrived here at 10.30 last night, 12½ hours non stop and, as you can guess, we were all dead beat. What a journey! 350 miles in one day on lorries! Still, today hasn't been too bad as I have managed to get a long sleep in. Well sweetheart, it seems that I stand a good chance of getting my month's leave within six weeks! So that isn't bad at all is it? Not too long for us to count the hours to. I felt very miserable and depressed on the way back darling and was thinking about you all the time ...

Berlin isn't too bad although we are a long way from the town ... By the way I have got my medal ribbons now dear: The 1939–1945 Star (red, light blue, dark blue). The Italy Star (red, white and green). The French German Star (red, white and blue) and the African Star (blue, yellow, red and light blue). So we are now walking around looking like miniature rainbows, very dazzling and bad for the eyes! ...

Good night sweet.

Your ever loving husband,

Ray. x x x x x x

P.S. I love you.

On the next day, 21 July, at ten o'clock there was a triumphant victory parade in Berlin, commencing with a 19-gun salute in honour of Winston Churchill. The 7th Armoured Division took a major part in the parade. Union Jacks were hoisted and every piece of equipment polished until it gleamed.

Field Marshall Sir Alan Brook, Sir Bernard Montgomery and Churchill progressed down the Charlottenburger Chaussee with their troops in attendance. There was an inspection and then march-past whilst the bands celebrated the courage, bravery and unfailing dedication of all who had fought in all the Campaigns, in Africa, Italy, France, Holland, Belgium and Germany. Ray, as a Desert Rat, had contributed to every single one.

On 22 July Ray writes again, but there is no mention of the victory parade. The rejoicing was overshadowed by a tragic accident:

> *... while I was on leave, one of my pals was drowned in a local canal while swimming. I was thunderstruck when I heard about it and, of course, very upset as I knew him very well and he was a very close friend of mine ... He would have been out of the army this year too. It is really very tragic after being with the Div. all these long years, to go out like that. Anyway we are making a collection for his widow to help her out a bit ...*

26.7.45.

My own darling wife,

... Berlin is very quiet indeed and absolutely nothing to be bought. I suppose you have read in the papers about the extensive Black Market activities going on here but the authorities are making a very big drive against this now and there is a general tightening up all round. I haven't been able to buy anything in the way of dress material or stockings yet.

You can't imagine how desolate everybody and everything is here. You cannot seem to buy anything at all except at ridiculous prices so 'they've had me' ...

The weather is glorious, real summer and very hot indeed ... I am missing you terribly darling, roll on my next leave! Well, it certainly seems as though Labour are sweeping the board doesn't it? Let's hope they will soon get cracking on this demobbing ...

2.8.45.

... Well darling, I heard some good news this morning. Just listen to this: They have increased the month's overseas service leave to six weeks! ... Instead of getting thirty days I shall get forty two!...

We can't grumble at the moment. We are getting very good

food, comfortable billets and no parades, so things are not so bad.

The weather hasn't been too kind lately, very stormy and rainy. The heatwave definitely appears to have gone. I am terribly busy at the moment still on the postal job. Everybody seems to be getting more letters than ever …

We had a very pleasant evening here last week with a barrel of beer and a piano. I wish you could have been there darling, you would have laughed. We happened to be short of drinking glasses and finished up by drinking out of salad bowls and small goldfish bowls! …

7.8.45.

… I shall be coming on my six weeks leave directly the regular post corporal comes back. … I believe we land at Tilbury and from there we have to go to Cobham in Surrey where we are paid out and given our ration cards etc., though I don't believe we are kept there long.

If, however, I happen to leave here in a rush and it's too late to write and let you know, I will send a wire directly we land …

It is probably the only time in my army career that I am glad I have so much overseas service. Anyway it's certainly better than a meagre seven or eleven days when you are looking at the clock every five minutes …

9.8.45.

… I expect to leave Berlin next Tuesday August 14th for my six weeks leave … I think it will take us about five days to get home, so I should be seeing you round about Aug. 19th or 20th. Anyway, I will send a wire when I know definitely dearest. …

P.S. I can't believe it's true, six weeks!

A telegram sent from Waterloo Station on 17 August states:

HOME TONIGHT LOVE RAY

A few days before Ray came home on leave, the situation in Japan was developing into a crisis. Wanting to expand her empire, she had conquered all the great islands lying between Asia and Australia. In May and June 1942, the Americans, having halted the Japanese advance, were fighting both Japan in the Pacific and Germany in Europe. Although they continued to bomb Japan, they decided to concentrate on Germany first. As soon as Germany was defeated, America was ready to invade Japan. She had been warned by both America and Britain that if she continued to fight, the atom bomb would be used. One was exploded at Hiroshima on 6 August killing 80,000 people and a second at Nagasaki on 9 August killing 40,000. On 14 August Japan surrendered.

Chapter 18

Return to Germany

A postcard written on 29 September reveals that Ray travelled to Sunningdale after his leave.

Sunningdale
Saturday 29th Sept.

Darling,
Just a few lines to let you know I arrived O.K. I saw my pal at King's X all right. As I expected, I think the squadron have moved again so don't write until you hear from me. Also another rumour of interest is that all groups up to 27 are leaving the Division. Whether that's any pointer for the demob. speed up I don't know. Anyway I've got my fingers crossed. Must close now darling as we may be sailing today. All my love and God Bless,
Ray. x x x x x x

An undated letter follows from Ostend.

Darling,
... I haven't yet arrived back to the squadron. I am writing this from Ostend and we hope to be leaving here today ... there is no need for me to say how much I am missing you dearest. The army does seem strange after such a long leave ...

I hope the wardrobe and divan have arrived O.K. and also the units.

Well sweetheart I shall have to close quickly as we may be moving off soon ...

God Bless dearest,

Ray. x x x x x x

Ray sends another letter on 5 October (his 32nd birthday).

Darling,
Well here I am once again still not yet back at the unit. We left Ostend yesterday and arrived at yet another transit camp. We hope to get straight to the Div. from here, although I don't suppose we shall get away before Sunday or Monday ...

Ray arrives three days later.

7911536 L/CPL HARRIS R.
H.Q. SQUADRON, 7TH ARMOURED DIV.
B.A.O.R.

8.10.45.

My own darling wife,
I arrived back at the squadron today after a somewhat tedious journey. The above address is correct dear so will you address all your letters accordingly?

I have found a few changes here already. The Sergeant Major is now an Officer and, of course, things seem a bit different after being so long away. It appears that all men up to group 31 will be leaving here during the next month or so. Where they will go I don't know. Thank goodness I shall soon be out for good. Everybody here seems browned off and, of course, very disappointed about the squadron being split up. Group 20 have already had their medical for demob. so it shouldn't be long now ...

It seems years since I left you darling; still, as long as the next few weeks go as quickly as my leave did, I shan't mind. At least we did a good bit of work getting the flat didn't we? It's nice to know that we have a little place of our own ...

Well, I suppose I shall have to start sorting the old kit out ...

Your ever loving husband,

Ray. x x x x x x

P.S. I love you, and am missing you terribly darling.

As Ray mentions, during his leave, he and Doreen had managed to start renting a flat (3 Albert Road, Brighton). It was on the second floor and Rex and Dorothy rented the top one. For the next three months Ray spent much time looking for suitable furnishings and taking a great interest in those that Doreen was able to buy.

In his next letter (12 October 1945) Ray tells Doreen that:

Some of our lads tell me that they have found it literally impossible to get a home of any kind.

He also hopes:

... this dock strike doesn't make any difference to the demob ... some people don't know when they are well off. It certainly shakes me. I see they have had to put the army unloading the food boats. The boys take the can back every time don't they? ... I miss you more each day darling.

On 15 October 1945 Ray reveals:

I am still doing the post job ... The Sergeant Major told me today that I shall not be leaving the squadron along with the others so it appears that I shall stay on here until I am demobbed. I am glad in a way. After all I haven't much longer to do now, so I may as well stay put here. However, most of the lads will be going and they are only retaining a few key men ...

On 19 October 1945 he encourages Doreen to buy half a tea

set, and to get the bell and a faulty light switch in the hall fixed. He says that:

> *The squadron here doesn't seem the same somehow since I've come back, too many changes and too many new faces. I don't think I shall ever be really settled here again ... am inclined to get a bit restless ... I am loving you and missing you always darling.*

On 22 October 1945 Ray tells Doreen he is sending two china, hand-painted cake sets home and he is on the lookout for a carpet.

> *They seem pretty scarce round here. Oh for Berlin again!*

Curiously he doesn't reveal exactly where he is stationed. The difficulty of setting up home after the war is suggested in the next letter (25 October 1945).

> *I was pleased to hear that the units had arrived at last. Well darling, a pal of mine here told me that when his units came, they allowed him 60 and he spent them all on his first order. Is this possible?*

On 28 October 1945 all Ray's energies continue to be directed towards 3 Albert Road. He had:

> *managed to get hold of an electric tone arm pick up and electric motor turntable. It's really a smashing job and brand new ... We will be able to convert the old gramophone and wireless into a radiogram. I was lucky to get hold of it ... for next to nothing, just a few shillings in fact ...*

This letter has an extra page attached headed:

> *'LATE EXTRA NEWS'*
>
> *Darling ... I have just met someone who may be able to get a*

carpet for me. I am seeing him tomorrow ... to talk on the terms ... I have made arrangements for a pal of mine (who is coming home on leave to England) to take it for me. I have instructed him to put it on the railway so it will come down to Brighton by passenger train addressed to No. 3 ... I hope it won't be too heavy for my pal to lug around ...

Another letter is written the same day saying there is a delay concerning the carpet so:

I shall bring it myself when I get demobbed. After all a few of the lads will give me a hand.

The news on 30 October 1945 is:

I'm afraid 'we've had' the carpet. I couldn't come to terms with the owner ... The latest 'griff' on the demob. of 24 group is that we are due at embarkation ports on Dec. 24th, so it looks as though our Xmas will be just a little late ... I have handed over the post job now and am taking over the squadron canteen ...

1.11.45.

My own darling wife,

... I have just finished packing [the teaset], *four parcels altogether ...*

Tomorrow is a big day here in the squadron as we are having our farewell 'binge' together with a few of the old 'Strollers' band (including Ronnie Vaughan).

I have promised to do a little act and one of the lads is also taking flashlight photos of the show. Yes, it's going to be quite a 'do'.

In the afternoon there is a comic football match between ... a team comprising the old lads of Western Desert days and ... new arrivals in the squadron. I think there are going to be a few laughs and probably a few minor injuries. No! I'm not playing.

What, group 24? No thanks! However, I will do my share in the evening show.

Well darling, today is the first of Nov. and it's nice to know that I shall be out <u>next</u> month. Yesterday all men's names in 23 and 24 groups appeared in orders for release. It was certainly good to see my name there and I certainly have waited a long time for it.

Winter is creeping in over here, very foggy, damp and miserable. I'm afraid the German people are going to have a hard time. Thank goodness I shall soon be away from it all.

Well dearest, my other 200 cigs. arrived yesterday, just the job!

I'm glad to hear ... you had a nice time at 'Smokey Joes', I could go one of those suppers right now, still it won't be long.

I'm afraid I shall have to close up now sweetheart, canteen manager these days and bags of account books to settle up, so I will say 'Goodnight Sweetheart' ...

4.11.45.

... Our farewell binge ... has been and gone. It went over really terrific and was a great success ... I had an enormous fur coat on for my act, a real Max Miller effort and am certainly looking forward to seeing the photos ...

Needless to say we all got horribly drunk. I lost count of the drinks I had. We all had a grand time, even if we are paying for it in 'hangovers'. Still it was our last 'do' together, so we had to make it a good one ...

6.11.45.

... Yesterday I wrote to my friend George Wilson of the Egyptian State Broadcasting to see if I can obtain the records of an early 'Jerboa Strollers' broadcast ...

Well darling it appears that groups 23 <u>and</u> 24 are having their release medical inspections together here. I expect mine on

Nov. 13th. It's certainly a step nearer isn't it darling? Boy! It's certainly getting cold out here these days and we are still doing P.T. exercises at 7.30 every morning. Still, I don't worry; every one is nearer to the end ...

8.11.45.

... Sorry to hear about your cold darling. Please be careful won't you dear. I do hope that by the time you get this dearest, you will be completely well again ... I started yet another new job today, N.C.O. in charge of petrol, so I am well occupied once again ...

I am missing you terribly darling more and more each day. I am praying for the one day to come when I can say 'Hello darling! Home for good!'

I don't think I can realise even now, (although it's so close), what it will mean, no more long partings for us dearest, together for always. We have everything before us and we will be able to start 1946 on the right foot and start living our own lives ...

The next letter (11 November 1945) reveals that Ray has bought two '*real hand-painted wall plates*' and '*a buff china coffee pot with milk and sugar basin to match*'. He writes:

... so with the 'pick up' as well to carry, I shall be pretty well loaded. ... I am having my shoes soled and heeled out here and will probably send them home just before I leave ...

P.S. Not many more letters to write now darling. I shall soon be telling you I LOVE YOU.

Rxxxxxx

13.11.45.

... The weather here has been terrible, raining every day. I don't go very far these days. We have very comfortable billets here, so generally bank the old fire up, turn the radio on and start reckoning up the days to Dec. 24th.

Sometimes, however, I stray down to the canteen for a game of table tennis (tell Rex to look out when I come home, I'm getting quite an expert) ... I am pretty busy these days with the petrol job, as besides issuing it, I also have to do the ledger work. Still, I don't mind, it passes the time and I don't do any guards ...

P.S. Only 41 days left now darling.

Poignantly, in the original letter, Doreen's eager wait is recorded by her marking off the days in faint pencil under the 41.

15.11.45.

... Well dear, I'm glad the cake sets arrived O.K. Sorry the four cups were broken. Were the white plates and saucers O.K.? I had my medical yesterday. Everything O.K. darling, graded A1 as usual ...

Well darling, roll on Dec. ... I didn't think a month could take so long to go by as Nov. is doing ...

In the next letter (18 November 1945) Ray tells Doreen that he is preparing some material for a show, to be performed for Cambrai Day.

... At the moment I am writing out a comedy sketch for another 'do' on Tues. night. Tuesday is known in the R.A.C. as Cambrai Day. I think it is named after the Battle of Cambrai, during the last war when British tanks went into action for the first time. Anyway, it is a big day for us and is celebrated accordingly. I shall be doing another act, but I think 'they've had me' as far as the 'hooch' is concerned. I haven't recovered properly from the last 'do' yet ...

It is getting bitterly cold here now and we are expecting the snow any time now ...

20.11.45.

My own darling wife,

... I have just come back from the Cambrai 'do', not quite as hectic as the last one, but quite enjoyable and I have finished up sober, two beers and a tea. That was my ration, so you can see I have been very steady darling. I have enclosed a photo of myself doing my single comedy act, not bad. What do you think darling? What a night that was and what a lovely audience. I had them all singing my signature tune at the end, 'I Wanna Go Back in the Evening'. It was a real farewell 'do' that evening and some of the lads were nearly in tears. Anyway, it's nice to think that there is still a little sentiment left even in the toughest of them.

I may (I said may) fix a deal over a carpet tomorrow darling and, if successful, have arranged for a pal of mine to bring it home for me.

He will put it on the train at Victoria for Brighton so it will be delivered to you by a railway lorry.

24.11.45.

... I hope you have got the ... carpet ... Although it's not particularly big, it is a good one darling but may be a little damp, so could you air it dear directly you get it ...

25.11.45.

... A new telegram service is operating between England and here and it is not expensive. It is called 'Postagram' and you can send one from any post office in England. It is very quick indeed and will reach me within 24 hours ...

Well darling, I was very sorry to hear that Eddie has got to go abroad. I can't understand it at all ... it doesn't seem worthwhile seeing that he is due for demob. in March or perhaps before if the speed up comes along ...

P.S. I LOVE YOU DARLING.

Our tank tracks lead from Cambrai,
Through mud and slush and rain,
O'er sand and wasted vastness
Through blood and fear and pain
Through all that grim array
The stench of foetid war,
Through all the martial clamour,
We greet the green once more.

And so we take our colours,
The Brown, the Red, the Green,
They stand for all our glory,
They stand for what has been,
But not only in their station
An honour to our name,
They also urge us onwards,
To further deeds of fame.

The Tank Corps Rat has brought us
From Cairo to Matruh,
From Sofafi to the Sunset
Of War out on the blue
From Italy to Blighty,
From Blighty to the Seine,
Onward then through Belgium,
To chase the Hun again

Till last we sit in Deutschland,
The green fields won at last,
With the laurels of our battles,
And the glory of our past.

R.D.A. Wills.

MENU

We hope to give you something good,
By purchase, shot or ravage,
But really you must understand,
That most depends on Savage.

Until the great day dawns, then,
We cannot really view,
What stocks exist for our delight,
Or write a Me and you

When all is said we hope to give
You soup upon your platter,
But if it doesn't happen thus,
Please don't complain or natter.

Fish as well is on our list,
Whatever it may be,
Hake or Skate or anything,
That swims beneath the sea.

Ah! Venison now das ist gut,
Mit Spuds and ander dinks,
We hope to give you for your fill,
(Or so Vic Lambert thinks)

To polish off this good array
A sweet to put your back up,
And then push back your plate and say,
"I've had enough, I'll pack up!"

Of course there's lots of beer and drinks
To swill the eats away,
To enliven the proceedings,
(And to make you sore next day).

R.D.A. Wills.

H. Q.
7th ARMOURED DIVISION

The Cambrai Day souvenir.

27.11.45.

My own darling wife,

... Tomorrow I am posting three more small rugs off. Now darling these want cleaning but they should come up very nice with carpet soap. Like the other they are rather small but of good quality and would cost a bit of money to buy nowadays. Later on I shall also be posting off two more mats, which will look nice in the bedroom or front room. Whichever you prefer darling. Unfortunately I have had to swap the coffee pot and two plates which I had darling for these rugs and mats. I don't think I could have managed to get the china home dear without breaking it and, after all, the rugs and mats are worth much more ...

As you can guess darling, I am dashing round getting all I can for our home. I still haven't given up hope of a big carpet yet and am still trying darling ...

Tomorrow we are signing our release papers etc. It's getting close now, eh darling? Not much longer now with November nearly over and Dec. will be my very last month in the army ... Goodnight sweetheart.

29.11.45.

... This morning I sent off another small carpet darling, by post...

Well dearest, tomorrow is the last day of Nov. thank goodness. I've never known such a long month. It's simply dragged. Still, it's a wonderful thought! December is my last month in the army and I shall be back with you darling for always. We are getting snow thick and heavy now, real Xmas weather! It looks nice while it's here but not so good when it starts to go, plenty of mud! ...

Your ever loving husband,

Ray. x x x x x x

Chapter 19

The Last Month

1.12.45.

My own darling,

... It has been a lovely sunny day here and I hope it has been the same at Brighton. Fancy dearest, only about 24 days to do now. I can hardly realize it. Let's hope those last few days will go quickly for both of us. Now dear, how will you manage as regards money when you leave Clutterbucks?[19] *I shan't be home until a week or two after you leave, and even if I make an extra allowance now, it won't come through until a fortnight or so ...*

Just made myself a cup of tea while writing this. Not so good as the old 'brews' at No. 3 though. I am certainly looking forward to those, also fish and chips, not forgetting the pickles! I am still looking for a large carpet darling, but, as we are only allowed to bring home 56lbs of kit including army stuff, it makes things a bit awkward. Anyway, I will get what I can ...

The next letter (2 December 1945) bears a postscript:

Not many more 'Goodnights' on paper now darling.
R. x x x x x x

19 Doreen's last place of work before Ray came home

5.12.45.

My own darling,

... Well dearest the latest news about group 24 is that we are leaving here in <u>two</u> lots, the first going on Dec. 28th and the next on Jan. 4th (not so good!). Still, let's hope that I am lucky enough to be in first. Anyway, I think I will. Meanwhile, as you can probably guess, I am counting the days now. I suppose it's a silly thing to do, as the time definitely drags that way, don't you think so darling? Still roll on the next three weeks. Nothing exciting going on here these days, except of course, I believe the squadron will soon be on a <u>peace time</u> basis, and I know what that means, bags of discipline, drills and parades. Thank goodness I'm getting out. I had a game of football yesterday, which we just managed to win 3-2. It was more of a comedy match really though and the ground pretty muddy.

Ray (on left) playing in a comedy football match.

I wish you could have seen it darling, it was a riot. Everybody was sliding up and down between the goals. The first goal was very funny and a lucky one for me. I got hold of the ball from about twenty yards out and slammed it hard. The goal keeper was standing near a big puddle of water, so you can guess what happened. The ball went straight into it and blinded the goalie with water. He was groping about (looking for group 26 I think) and it just trickled into the net. The lads roared, you can imagine it can't you? I think we all spent more time on the ground than standing up ...

Well dearest, it certainly looks as though our Xmas and New Year together will be a little late.

Don't forget to look out for the other things I sent by post dear ... I can see the old carpet soap in action when I get home again. Remember the last time darling? What a game, still I love messing around doing little things like that and I hope they haven't sold all the dark stain at the corner shop.

By the way darling, I dropped Lawsons a line the other day asking for all particulars and what salary they were prepared to pay me. I told them I would be ready to start after three or four weeks leave so I am waiting a reply. Nothing like getting these things fixed is there dear? I am enclosing the Cambria Day souvenir, also a photo of the old Div. Axis in Berlin. I thought you may like to look at them.

Well sweetheart I shall have to close up once again now with all my love and kisses. Goodnight dearest and God Bless.

Soon be with you now.

Your ever loving husband,

Ray. x x x x x x

THIS AXIS
HAS BEEN
LAID FROM
EL ALEMEIN TO BERLIN
VIA:-
AFRICA
TOBRUK
BENGHAZI
TRIPOLI
MARETH
TUNIS
ITALY
SALERNO
NAPLES
VOLTURNO
FRANCE
NORMANDY
THE SEINE
ROUBAIX
BELGIUM
OUDENARDE
GHENT
MALINES
HOLLAND
EINDHOVEN
TILBURG
THE MAAS
GERMANY
THE RHINE
AHAUS
SULINGEN
NIENBURG
SOLTAU
HAMBURG
AXIS
THE END OF A LONG TRAIL.

The 7th Armoured Division Axis.

The next letter, dated 7 December 1945, mentions a settee:

> *... It's a great pity about the settee isn't it? I suppose we had better have brown rexine don't you think darling? I wish we had*

known before. If you remember, I could have got a brown rexine suite to match for £25. Do you remember the advert darling? Have Jay's got a specimen of this rexine settee on show dear? If so, and you like it darling, I should let the order go through. I shouldn't under any circumstances order one without seeing it first dear. After all, you know what these firms are, especially Jay's ...

Well dearest, I was surprised to hear that Donald Peers is playing the old 'Hipp.'.[20] *It is his first visit to Brighton, I think anyway. I hope you liked him and the show. Yes darling, the days are going slowly but surely and we haven't long to wait before we are together for always. It sounds grand doesn't it dearest, always! ...*

Two days later (9 December 1945) Ray writes:

... I have just sent another carpet (small) off by post and have registered it, so you should get it a little quicker. Before sending it I cleaned it with a little petrol so don't put it by the fire to air will you dear, in case it isn't entirely evaporated. It's quite a good one dear but is very slightly worn, although not noticeable and should look even better with a little carpet soap. I also heard from Dad at No. 4 and was very pleased to hear that Eddie may not go abroad after all ...

The next letter bears disappointing news:

10.12.45.

... Well dearest it appears that 24 group will not be leaving here until Jan. 5th and this is official, worse luck!

The trouble is that we are coming out at an awkward time as all demob. centres and sailing are at a standstill over Xmas, so that holds up things a bit. It takes about four days from when we leave here till we are actually demobbed, so it will be about the 9th darling. I was hoping to make it for Jan. 2nd or 3rd. Still

20 Brighton Hippodrome

there it is dear and it can't be helped. All the lads in 24 group are very disappointed here, as you may guess. Never mind, we will make up for it darling when I get home. After waiting five and a half years, six more days won't make all that difference after all. I heard from Lawsons today and they want me to go up to their London Office during my leave to talk things over. Still that can wait a bit.

By the way dear, I am sending the divisional Xmas card. It's not so good this year, in fact, a bit ropey I think. I am only allowed <u>*two*</u> *of these and the other one I am sending to No. 4 ...*

P.S. I love you darling!

The card Ray mentions shows two rats, one dressed in uniform and one dressed in 'civvies', shaking hands in farewell. Ray has added to the picture:

It won't be long now darling!

14.12.45.

... Well dearest there's no need for me to tell you how impatient I am getting here, waiting to get away on that last one way journey home. Nearly all the old lads here have been posted away now, so the squadron is more or less entirely new now.

It will certainly be a strange sight at the Xmas spread this year, after seeing the old faces every year for so long. The system has changed a bit now too, a bit more discipline and a few more parades etc. Still it won't be long now till I am saying 'au revoir' to it all ...

Goodnight darling and God Bless.

<u>*One more night nearer*</u> *...*

The next letter, dated 16 December 1945, mentions some photographs which Ray has had taken (they would have cost 15/- each to be done in England). Ray also writes that he has heard from Eddie's mother, Mrs. Lane. He had sent her some bulbs, which he hoped would not develop into marrows!

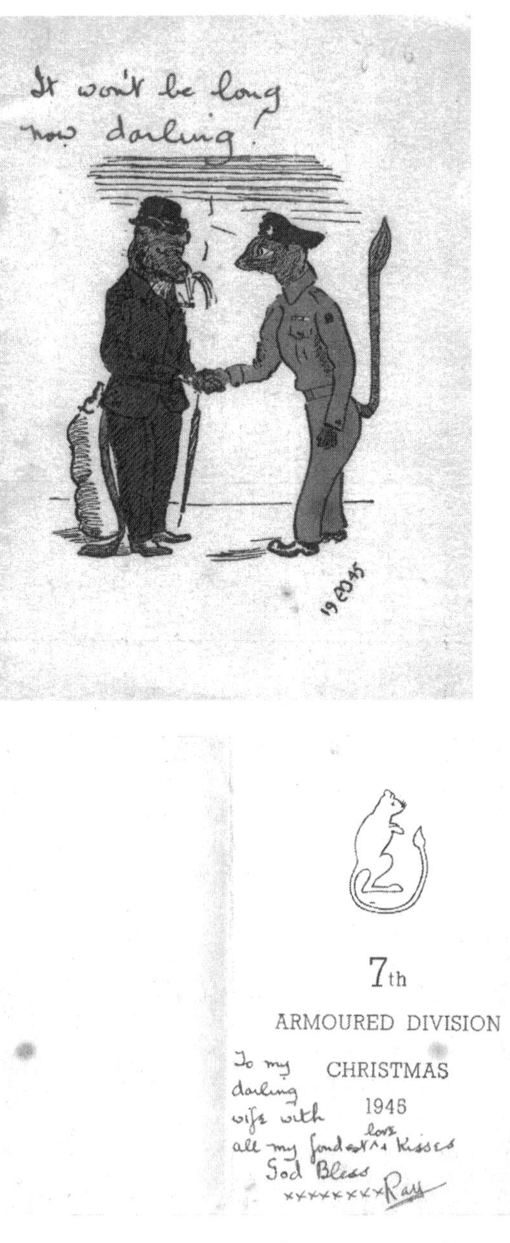

The 7th Armoured Division Christmas Card, 1945.

18.12.45.

... Even if I am not with you on Xmas Day darling, you know I shall be thinking of you every minute sweetheart and praying for the last few days to go quickly, so that I can be with you for always ... Once again I am putting on another Xmas show this year and, of course, with all the new lads in, I shall use a lot of my old gags and patter, so it is not so difficult as usually is the case. Well darling I will finish up this time by wishing you a very, very Happy Xmas my dearest, I shall be thinking of you ...

On the same day, Ray writes a second letter to announce some good news:

18.12.45.

... I have just written to you dear and posted the letter.

Since then I have just learned that I shall be leaving here for demob. on Dec. 29th and not on Jan. 5th. That means I should land up in B'ton round about Jan. 2nd or 3rd. So that's a bit better isn't it darling? It also means eight days less for me to wait. As you guess dear, I am very bucked about it ...

20.12.45.

My own darling wife,

... Just fancy darling, only just over a week now and I shall be away from here.

Of course, we have to go through various stages before we are actually demobbed but I should be home by 2nd or 3rd, anyway, I will send a wire from Guildford, as I believe that is where I go. Well darling I am very busy with rehearsals at the moment of writing, in fact, I am expecting a few of the lads round any moment to run through a sketch I am putting on.

By the way dear, many thanks for the Xmas card received today. It was very nice. Well darling, I don't know when you will receive this letter but I don't think it will be much good your writing back, as I shall probably be gone and on my way home. The postal service is bound to be bad over Xmas, and mail held up for days, so I should hang on for my wire to arrive. Darling, I can hardly realize this will probably be the last letter I shall write to you. In under a fortnight I shall be Mr. Harris, wonderful thought!

Well! The lads have arrived for rehearsal, so I will close now darling, with all my fondest love and kisses. Goodnight darling and God Bless, in haste,

Your ever loving husband,

Ray. x x x x x x

This isn't, in fact, Ray's final letter. He writes two more. The first, two days later.

22.12.45.

My own darling wife,

Just a few more lines dear. Well, a week today, I leave here for demob.. Getting very close now eh! darling?

Today, I am handing my kit in, all except what I am allowed to keep, namely shirts, one battledress, boots and underwear etc. So my real soldiering days are more or less finished. The big thing here at the moment (apart from demob. of course) is our variety show, which I am putting on, on Xmas Day. It will be my last, so I want it to be good. It should turn out all right. Anyway I will tell you all about it when I see you darling. Well dear, look out for the wire which I will send directly I know for certain which day I shall arrive.

As I mentioned before, barring cancellations, I should be home demobbed by Jan. 2nd or 3rd. I am counting the hours now until the end darling, the end of a very long road. Excuse short letter darling, but still very busy on the show dear and I haven't a lot of time left between now and Xmas Day, so will close now, with all my fondest love and kisses.

Goodnight and God Bless darling,

Your ever loving husband,

Ray. x x x x x x

Ray entertaining at the final Demob. Concert, December 1945.

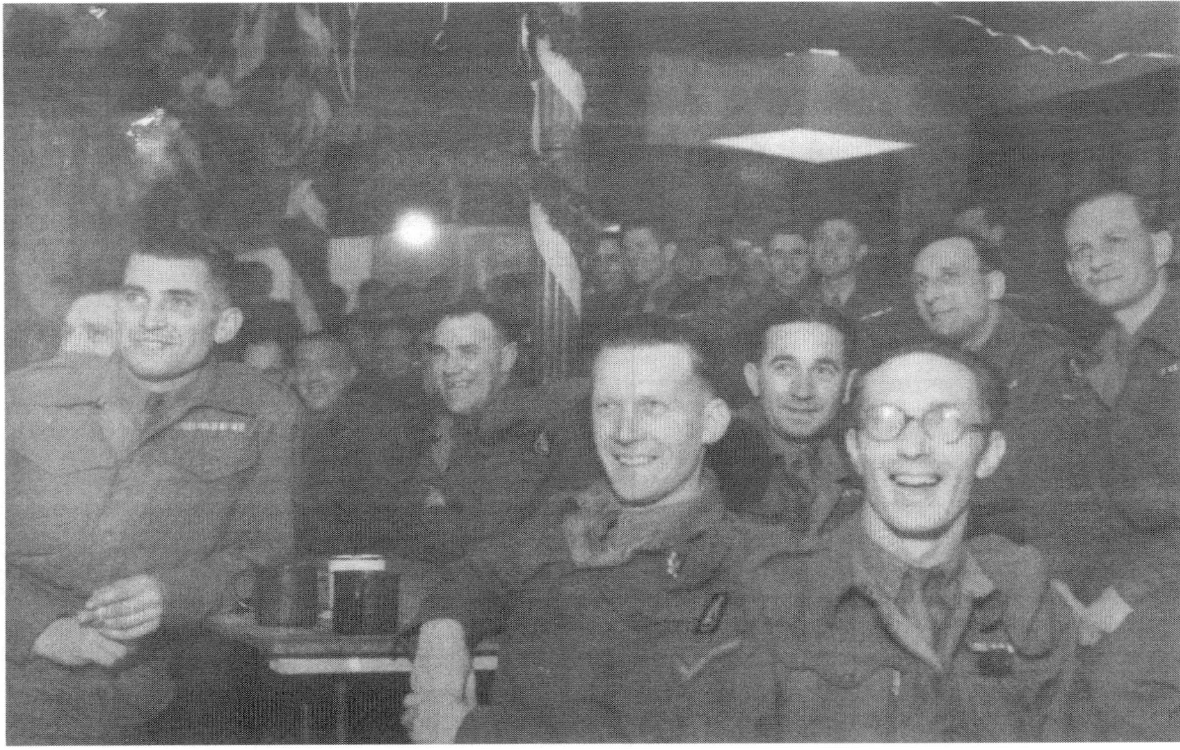

The audience watching Ray's act at the final Demob. Concert, December 1945.

7911536. L/CPL. HARRIS. R.
HQ SQN. 7TH ARMOURED DIV
B.A.O.R.
26.12.45.

My own darling wife.

So glad to hear that you received my letter telling you that I am leaving here on the 29TH. Yes darling, its wonderful news isn't it? less than three days to do now. Well, we have got over the Xmas celebrations O.K and we had quite a nice do. The show went over big as usual, and everything went off with a swing.

(2)

Like you dear, I'm afraid that I couldn't really concentrate, all my thoughts were with you and the 29TH. We had a fairly warm Xmas for a change, a bit different from last year, when we were up to our necks in snow and ice. Well darling, I hope you had a nice time over the holiday. I kept very sober this time, 1 whiskey, 1 gin, and a couple of beers. I seem right off it these days, can't seem to stomache it at all.

Pages 1 & 2 of Ray's last letter to Doreen from Germany, (26.12.1945).

③

I think our first farewell party taught me a lesson, I haven't been the same since. There were plenty of drinks to be had however, and the young lads (groups 40 – 60) revelled in it. Needless to say after about half an hour of mixing them, they were falling out like flies, and cut a very sorry picture this morning. Well, I don't know how long this letter will take to reach you darling, I may possibly arrive first anyway, I will send the

④

wire directly I know for sure which day I shall be home.

Shall have to close now dear with all my love & kisses once again.

Goodnight dear, and God Bless.

Your ever loving husband
Ray
xxxxxxxxxxxxxxxxxxxxxxxxxxxxxxxx

PS Get that cup of tea ready darling.
Brighton here I come!

Ray

Pages 3 & 4 of Ray's last letter to Doreen from Germany, (26.12.1945).

Ray's release book judged his military conduct as 'exemplary'. The testimonial reads:

One of the hardest working and least rewarded men in this squadron. A duty N.C.O. who could very easily have carried a third stripe had there been a vacancy. A keen dabbler in Amateur Theatricals.

Every man on demobilisation received a personal message from the commander of the 7th Armoured Division, Major General L. O. Lyne. It congratulated each Desert Rat on his dedicated service, his unfailing courage and his bravery in the Middle East, the victory of Alamein, Tunis, the Italian Campaign, Western Europe, Normandy, the crossing of the Rhine, the advance into Germany and the final occupation of Hamburg.

Ray's final letter is written on Boxing Day.

7911536 L/CPL HARRIS, R.
H.Q. SQN., 7th ARMOURED DIV.,
B.A.O.R.

26.12.45.

My own darling wife,
So glad to hear that you received my letter, telling you that I am leaving here on the 29th. Yes, darling, it's wonderful news isn't it? Less than three days to do now! Well we have got over the Xmas celebrations O.K. and we had quite a nice 'do'. The show went over big as usual and everything went off with a swing. Like you dear, I'm afraid that I couldn't really concentrate. All my thoughts were with you and the 29th. We had a fairly warm Xmas for a change. A bit different from last year, when we were up to our necks in snow and ice. Well darling, I hope you had a nice time over the holiday. I kept very sober this time, 1 whisky, 1 gin and a couple of beers. I seem right off it these days, can't seem to stomach it at all. I think our first farewell party taught

me a lesson. I haven't been the same since. There were plenty of drinks to be had, however, and the young lads (groups 40–60) revelled in it.

Needless to say, after about half an hour of 'mixing' them, they were falling out like flies and cut a very sorry picture this morning.

Well, I don't know how long this letter will take to reach you darling. I may possibly arrive first anyway. I will send the wire directly I know for sure which day I shall be home.

Shall have to close now dear with all my love and kisses once again.

Goodnight dear and God Bless.

Your ever loving husband,

Ray. x x x x x x

P.S. Get that cup of tea ready darling!

BRIGHTON, HERE I COME!

POST OFFICE

TELEGRAM

No. 974

Charges to pay
s. d.
RECEIVED

Prefix. 35 Time handed in. Office of Origin and Service Instructions. Words.

At 4.52 m

From

By

OFFICE STAMP
BRIGHTON
ARRIVED

At m
To
By

435 4.18 FOLKESTONE SCE PTY 11

HARRIS 3 ALBERT RD BRIGHTTN =

ARRIVED WED EXPECT HOME THURS = RAY

For free repetition of doubtful words telephone "TELEGRAMS ENQUIRY" or call, with this form at office of delivery. Other enquiries should be accompanied by this form, and, if possible, the envelope. B or C

CT 3

G.N.P.Co. Ltd. 51-6133

The telegram informing Doreen that Ray had arrived in England (02.01.1946).

Brighton 1946. Ray, his father, Doreen, Vera, Peter and cousin.

Epilogue

After the war, Ray successfully auditioned in London following an advertisement in *The Performer.* However, I was born in May 1947 and my sister Susan in September 1948.

Having a young family to support, Doreen and Ray felt that a career in show business would be too insecure. Variety shows did, in fact, rapidly disappear with the onset of television.

For many years Ray worked as a coach painter and later in freight development. His wonderful sense of humour and quick wit remained with him right up to his death in 2001 and family get-togethers were always full of warmth, joke telling and laughter.

Ray's advertisement in The Performer *which led to a successful audition.*

Acknowledgements

All "Southdown's" quotations are reproduced by kind permission of The World's Fair Ltd.

Many thanks to:

Val Ward for typing the original manuscript.

My brother-in-law Bill Smurthwaite for checking the historical details.

My husband Leon and sister Sue for all their encouragement and support.

The Evening Argus for the photo of Max Miller.

Indepenpress for making a dream come true.

About the Author

Jenny Hall (née Harris) was born and brought up in Brighton and Hove. In 1968 she qualified as a teacher in London and married Leon. A nomadic few years followed in Oxford, Sweden, France and Bath teaching English and studying classical ballet, modern dance and yoga, whilst Leon competed as an international high jumper.

They chose to settle in Crawley, Sussex (within easy reach of the Royal Opera House and Festival Hall!) where Jenny taught English as a second language in a middle school. Since retiring, she has learned to ballroom dance, continues to practise yoga and has had a number of poems published.